COOK YOURSELF A FAVOUR

A wealth of delicious and wholesome recipes for all occasions,
especially created to improve health and vitality, with menu suggestions
and valuable information on macrobiotic and wheat-free diets.

RUEN

Cook Yourself A FAVOUR

350 Recipes to Help YOU Help Yourself to Better Health

**Dr Sheila Gibson
Louise Templeton
and Dr Robin Gibson**

THORSONS PUBLISHING GROUP
Wellingborough * New York

First published in 1983 by Johnson Green & Co. Publishers Ltd. (Scotland)
This edition first published 1986

British Library in Publication Data

Gibson, Sheila L.M.
   Cook yourself a favour : 350 recipes to help
yourself to better health.
   1. Egg-free diet—Recipes 2. Milk-free diet—
Recipes 3. Wheat-free diet—Recipes
I. Title II. Templeton, Louise III. Gibson,
Robin G.
641.5'63   RM232

ISBN 0-7225-1320-8

Printed and bound in Great Britain

CONTENTS

ABOUT THE AUTHORS

Robin Gibson has qualifications in both medicine and dentistry, with specialist qualifications in child health and homoeopathy. He has been a consultant at the Glasgow Homoeopathic Hospital for the past thirteen years where he has initiated research in the fields of allergy and rheumatology. It was in the course of this work that he became increasingly aware of the importance of diet in health and disease.

Sheila Gibson is qualified in both medicine and biochemistry with a more recent degree in homoeopathy. She has been working with her husband for the past nine years and has become increasingly involved in the challenging problem of applying theoretical dietary considerations in an appealing but practical way.

Louise Templeton has qualifications in home economics, nutrition and dietetics. She has had practical experience, both in hospitals and in the community at large, in therapeutic dietetics and the training of catering staff in the preparation of special diets. Over the past twelve years she has combined interests in travel and nutrition, investigating nutrition therapy as applied in centres as far flung as Canada and North America, Scandinavia, continental Europe, North Africa and the Far East.

FOREWORD

There has been increasing evidence over the past twenty-five years that factors in our environment have much more to do with the occurrence and distribution of disease than we realized before. It is clear that of these environmental influences, dietary factors are of very great significance. This has brought a new importance, and therefore renewed interest on the part of doctors and dietitians alike, to the state of our knowledge of nutrition in general and habits of eating – that is individual dietary structure – in particular. This is a complex subject and clearly our state of knowledge at this time shows up many areas in which there is the necessity for further study and research. Enlightenment from this will progressively allow a proper understanding of the potential role of dietary structure in disease.

At the present time there is a correct emphasis by dietitians and doctors on a progressive but cautious attitude in respect of dietary advice and there is wisdom in an outlook of moderation in this regard. Nevertheless, the case for adequacy of dietary fibre is well established, as is the desirability that this fibre be retained within the food in its natural state rather than provided as supplements – although it is preferable to have fibre provided in this way rather than

do without it. Again, clearly, an excess of animal fats of all kinds has been shown adversely to affect the risk factors for arterial disease and its associations. Perhaps the most influential nutrient in its capacity to do harm is the one that is both cheap and the most readily available – sugar. Its insinuation into so many readily consumable products, like sweets and soft drinks, is rarely immediately appreciated.

As a predominantly meat-eating country, it is right for us to consider the role of excess meat consumption in disease, and in this respect it is not well enough appreciated that there is a large content of residual, saturated animal fat left, even after all visible fat has been removed from a joint. In the case of domesticated cattle, this can be as much as 40 per cent by weight. The role of an excess of animal protein in aggravating a tendency to gout is undisputed but there are also now adequate grounds for linking heavy meat consumption with increased risk of other diseases including obesity, renal stone and cardiovascular problems. Epidemiological evidence clearly shows benefits from the vegetarian style and this must surely indicate the advisability, if nothing more, of much greater moderation in the animal protein content of our daily diets.

Cattle, after all, are economically grossly wasteful in the terms of the land and the foodstuffs they require. A lesser dependence on meat would certainly mean our greater national self-sufficiency in food and release valuable grain products for others. There is no greater example than this of 'living more simply that others may simply live'.

This book clearly emphasizes the great variety there is in ways of eating which are much less dependent on meat. The simplicity of the recipes is a feature quite apart from their wholesomeness. The authors point out the capacity of certain foodstuffs to cause feelings, if not manifestations, of ill-health about which the individual may be quite unaware and which – by trial of the recipes in this book – he may come to know about by their subsequent omission. One such is wheat, and the authors have in mind that this is partly ascribable to degrees of gluten sensitivity or sensitization. Their philosophy is to be commended since there are probably many of us who are only vaguely and even unwillingly aware that certain foodstuffs do not agree with us.

Their advice in this book can only make us more aware and therefore more objective about what we eat.

The recipes sound delightful and I wish I could say that I had been able to try them already myself but this is not the case. Nevertheless I look forward to working my way progressively through the book! They include many things which are new to me, such as the seaweeds, and this and other constituents will intrigue many who read about these here. I have no doubt that natural curiosity will lead us all to try all of those foods with which we have so far been unfamiliar.

The style of the authors is pleasantly instructive and encouraging and the book will have a great appeal to those who are prepared to stand aside from the bustle of daily life and explore some things new when the time comes around for the preparation and cooking of food.

Professor N. J. Blacklock F.R.C.S.
University Hospital of South Manchester

INTRODUCTION

DIETS FOR HEALTH

Anyone who has ever tried to be healthy knows that it just doesn't happen by chance. Most people in the western world unconsciously spend a lot of time, effort and money on becoming ill. Those born with a strong constitution are usually the worst offenders, as they can abuse their systems for longer before they experience any obvious ill-effects. The weaker amongst us learn to be more careful or simply (or not so simply) die.

Others spend all their lives chasing after what seems to be an elusive state of well-being, trying out a variety of 'health diets' or 'health programmes' – everything from jogging to vitamin swallowing. Any benefits tend to be short in duration.

Some who have good bodily health do not know what to do with this priceless possession, except to get rid of it as quickly as possible. Consider, for instance, Mr T. who comes excitedly into his doctor's surgery.

'Thank you, doctor, for seeing me at such short notice, but I'm really worried.'

'Worried, Mr T.? And you look so well.'

'That's it, doctor. I knew you would notice it right away. I didn't sign on with you for nothing. It's looking so well that's worrying me doctor. It started about a month ago and it's already ruining my social life, and is threatening to break up my family. You've got to help me.'

'Just calm down, Mr T. Start at the beginning and tell me all about it.'

'Well, doctor, about three months ago I read this book. It talked about the foods that were nutritious, not just because of the vitamins and minerals, etc. that they contained, but because they were properly balanced to suit my personal make-up, occupation and lifestyle, and the climate in which I was living. It explained how my present state of ill-health was a result of my faulty eating and living habits.'

'Hold on a minute, Mr T. You mean it was one of those faddy "alternative" – what do they call them – holistic-type books?'

'It had been recommended by an awfully nice young couple who just moved in next door, so to be polite, I read it, and you know, doctor, it makes sense.'

'American, was it?'

'So I started to follow its guidelines, stopped smoking – well at least I cut down drastically – started walking places that I would have normally taken the car, changed to a more wholesome way of eating – cut out sugar, white flour, additives, all that sort of thing – and started eating brown rice, fresh vegetables, discovered a whole range of foods I never knew existed. At first I did miss the sweets, and the bacon for breakfast, and I had an awful week when I had one of the worst colds I could remember.'

'You were weakening yourself, no doubt.'

'But that's the odd thing, doctor. The next week it happened. I woke up one morning – at 6 a.m. – and said to myself – George, you're healthy – you're actually healthy! I felt great. No sinus – you know how I was a slave to my sinuses – no ache in my back. No need for that first cup of black coffee to get me going. A few deep-breathing exercises in the open air, a bowl of porridge, some toasted seeds, and I was ready for anything. At first I took it in my stride – I had had days of feeling OK in the past – but I had to admit, never all the time, or so OK. Gradually I had to admit that being healthy was beginning to worry me. My friends were noticing, my family couldn't understand why I refused to take them out for doughnuts, chips and sugary drinks any more. It's been a month now, doctor. I feel great and what really worries me is that apart from the worries I've just told you about, I am enjoying being healthy. Tell me, doctor, is there anything you can do for me?'

'Well, it's like this, Mr T. If you had walked in here with severe depression, angina, skin rash, hiatus hernia, or something, I would have had the prescription in your hands and you out of here in three minutes. But you are asking me a very difficult question. Health is one of those conditions that we in the medical profession know very little about. We are disease specialists, and as such, know an awful lot about ill-health. When you are surrounded by sick people that you can diagnose and prescribe for, it doesn't leave you all that much time to think about health – though there is some research going on at the moment into the subject somewhere. Every doctor dreads a moment like this, Mr T. All I can say to you

at present is that you are without doubt healthy, and you will just have to learn to live with it.'

DIETS GALORE ... SO WHY MORE?

To be more serious, however, many people feel that health is such an elusive commodity that they wonder if it really can be attained.

In recent years a multitude of books has appeared on the market, describing a host of different diets for such conditions as obesity, arthritis, multiple sclerosis, food allergies, the hyperactive-learning-disability syndrome, diets for super-vitality, diets for longevity, macrobiotic diets, and so on. So many have appeared that anyone might well be excused for challenging the necessity of yet another book on the subject.

Our main reason for writing this book is to try to create some order out of the chaos, and to examine, and hopefully clarify, the main contradictions and conflicting opinions that exist on the subject of diet. It is also to help our own patients who so frequently complain, when we advise a certain diet, that we are suggesting that they eat foods which other authorities have advised them never to take, and who ask how there can be so many contradictory ideas on what is used, apparently, to have been so simple a matter for our ancestors.

Certainly, the subject today is riddled with confusion. Some medical authorities deny that diet is of any importance in disease causation, while others advocate a variety of conflicting regimes for their patients. If the medical profession itself is confused, it is hardly surprising that their patients are also bewildered.

It is a sobering thought that the incidence of chronic disease in this country has gone up by leaps and bounds since the end of the Second World War. Epidemiologists noted that the incidence of a number of chronic degenerative conditions had been on the increase before the outbreak of war, but the rate has sharply increased since about the start of the 1950s. If diet indeed has a part to play in this, it might be instructive to look at what has happened to our food in the past three decades.

A number of degenerative conditions became more common shortly after the introduction of steel roller mills in the milling industry. For the first time a really white flour could be produced, though at the expense of removing virtually all of the fibre and a significant percentage of the trace minerals and vitamins from the grain.[1]

In the past three decades, an increasing number and variety of foods have been subjected to processing. Not only has there been an increase in the canning industry, but frozen and dehydrated foods, and a whole range of instant-snack products, have appeared on the market. Modern supermarket shelves groan beneath an ever-increasing array of instant and convenience foods which, alas, have been deprived of most of their vitamins and trace nutrients in the process. And not only that! To improve the appearance, palatability and shelf-life of these devitalized products, a whole range of synthetic colouring and flavouring agents, tenderizers, stabilizers and preservatives has been devised.

At the present time there are more than 4,000 additives which can find their way into our food, many of which have never been adequately tested for toxicity singly, let alone in the combinations likely to occur in the average 'supermarket' meal.

Horrifying as all this is, to one who sits down and seriously contemplates the eating habits of the western world, it is by no means the end of the story. Parallel with the chemicalization and processing of our food once it has been produced, there has also been an increased use of chemicals in agriculture, during food production. Increasing quantities of artificial fertilizers, herbicides and pesticides are being sprayed on the land, and not only is the amount increasing annually, but degradation of these chemicals can be slow, resulting in a build-up of levels in the soil from year to year.

In the face of the foregoing facts, it would be surprising if diet did *not* have a part to play in the increasing incidence of chronic degenerative disease and general ill-health which has been witnessed in the past thirty years.

Before we can consider what would constitute a healthy diet, it would be as well, firstly, to remember what our food is for. Basically, it has two functions:

1) To provide us with fuel, a process which requires a whole host of different enzymes;

2) To replace worn-out or 'lost' components such as protein, vitamins, minerals and trace elements, the building blocks of our bodies and the co-factors and aids required for the many enzymes which keep it functioning.

A healthy diet must therefore supply sufficient fuel and also sufficient components, vitamins, minerals and trace factors, to enable it to function smoothly. For top-class performance, these should be supplied in the proportions required by the body. Excess of any factor surplus to requirements has either to be stored, or excreted. Either is potentially harmful since the storage overloads, and the excretion overworks the system.

The modern-day factory-produced, refined, processed food provides us with plenty of fuel – too much in many instances – stored as fat – but is sadly deficient in many vitamins and trace nutrients. Thus the body is made to work hard, processing the surplus fuel, but is not given sufficient tools (vitamins, etc.) to do the job efficiently. No wonder it starts to break down or degenerate. There is also the problem of a whole array of artificial chemicals for which it has no use. Not only that, but in many instances it has no tools at all for dealing with these unnatural products which, if it cannot get rid of them, interfere with the microscopic organization of the cells and tissues and cause further inefficiency in the body's working.

It is the belief of the authors of this book that the chemical stress on the body caused by both pollution by unwanted, unnecessary, artificial chemicals, and lack of essential nutrients, is a root cause of much of the chronic degenerative ill-health seen today.

From this it follows that an obvious step to take in the creation of a healthy diet would be to cut out all refined and processed foods, i.e., refined white flour and white sugar products, from which the essential nutrients required for processing by the body have been removed. Most of these also contain chemical additives. Examples are sweets and bakery products – cakes, biscuits – and many tinned, packeted and bottled foods and drinks. Just for interest, you might like to assess what proportion of your local supermarket's shelves are devoted to such items. Food for thought indeed!

Cutting out these products means, basically, reverting to what our great-grandparents ate: fresh, whole food as it comes from the orchards and farms, food which comes to us direct, without going through a factory first. Such a diet goes a long way to restoring the body's balance, cutting out a number of useless chemicals and giving the body a better, and balanced, supply of the essential vitamins, minerals and trace elements. Remember that vitamin pills, whether bought in a health food shop or not, do not adequately fill this role, as the vitamins are present in arbitrary doses, not necessarily those which are optimal for the body. Also, taking one vitamin in large quantities may change the requirements of others in ways that are not yet fully understood.

Contrary to popular belief, it is possible to obtain from plant sources all the vitamins required by the body, apart from vitamin D. This latter can be supplied by the interaction of sunlight with the skin. The most reliable sources of vitamin B_{12} are animal proteins – meat, dairy produce, poultry, eggs and fish; but B_{12} is also produced by bacteria and fungi, and preparations of fermented grains and pulses such as miso, and also sea vegetables, contain useful amounts. (See Appendix 3, on page 133, for sources of vitamins and minerals.) Eating a wide variety of fresh foods is the best guarantee against nutrient deficiency.

Another step we can take is to try, as far as possible, to avoid those pollutants which enter our food during its production. This means choosing organically-grown grains, fruits and vegetables, rather than the commercially produced equivalent, and free-range instead of battery-produced eggs and poultry. In this connection, lamb is probably preferable to either beef or pork as it is less likely to have been fed on artificial feed supplements and injected with antibiotics, steroids and other drugs. Fish (apart from the fish farm variety) and game, are probably preferable to lamb for the same reasons.

Another source of confusion arises in connection with polyunsaturated fats. These are the vegetable oils, as opposed to the saturated animal fats. Some of the polyunsaturated oils are essential for the body as it cannot manufacture them itself, and these are termed the essential fatty acids. The health benefits of the polyunsaturated fats appear to be due entirely to their essential fatty acid content. Unfortunately, both the commercial extraction of vegetable oils and margarine production tend to change the structure of the essential fatty acids and so reduce the nutritional value of the oils.[2] Therefore, when buying vegetable oils, always choose the cold-pressed varieties which retain a high percentage of the essential fatty acids as well as vitamin E, which is a natural antioxidant, preserving the oil from rancidity. Unless a dairy-free diet is prescribed, butter is always recommended for sparing use in preference to margarine, which is a highly processed product.

Apart from these simple guidelines to eating whole, fresh, organically or naturally produced foods, and avoiding refined, processed, commercially produced ones, there is no single diet for health, nor are there any true 'health foods'. There is just a style or manner of eating which can improve health. It is not necessarily true that if a little of something is good, more is better. In many instances, too much is just as harmful as too little, both being unbalanced. What we are aiming for is harmony and balance, and a positive attitude to life can be as important as the nutrient composition of the diet. The foods required to help restore balance will vary with the individual, both with his own make-up, and with his initial state of imbalance.

Similarly, the requirements of the same individual will vary from time to time. The diet required to maintain the balance may be quite different to that required to restore the balance in the first place. From this it follows that there is never even a 'diet for life', but a flexible diet tailored to maintain the dynamic equilibrium of the body.

THE 'WHEAT-FREE' DIET

This diet was devised a number of years ago as an answer to one specific aspect of the food pollution problem, namely that associated with artificial fertilizers and/or agricultural sprays (herbicides, pesticides and fungicides). It was discovered that wheat was detrimental to a large number of our patients; and a significant proportion of them experienced improvements in their health if they avoided wheat in their diets. Rye, barley, oats and rice did not have this effect. Moreover, the problem was not inherent in wheat itself, as organically produced wheat was not harmful, whereas the commercially produced variety was. The logical inference was that the detrimental effect is associated with the difference between the organic and commercial methods of cultivation. Why non-organically produced rye, oats, barley and rice do not seem to be affected to the same extent as wheat is not yet known.

Clinically, we discovered that many people who did not feel well, but for whom no specific diagnosis could be made, could rapidly feel very much better simply by avoiding wheat in their diet, with no medication being required. So-called malingerers, people who were one or two degrees under par ('just not well, doctor'), those who always felt tired and had no energy, and lacked the ability to cope with life, suddenly found that life had taken on a new meaning. Patients with heart problems, gastro-intestinal complaints, migraines, skin problems and arthritis, also benefitted from the 'wheat-free' diet. This diet, it must be admitted, also avoids all processed foods simply because most of those foods contain wheat in some form or another as a bulker or filler. Mono-sodium glutamate (MSG), the commonly used 'flavour enhancer', is also prepared from wheat. If anyone doubts the prevalence of wheat and MSG in processed foods, then they should spend a little time reading the labels on the tins and packets on the local supermarket shelves (see Appendix 1, page 130).

However, all the advantages of the wheat-free diet cannot be obtained simply by avoiding processed foods and by eating fresh whole foods, if bread or other bakery products prepared from non-organically grown wheat, however wholemeal it may be, are also included in the diet. Bran, which is almost always produced from wheat, must also be avoided.

Since the first edition of this book was prepared in 1983, support for our theory of the detrimental effects of artificial fertilizers and biocide sprays (herbicides, pesticides and fungicides) has come from several independent sources. In an address given to the Annual General Meeting of the Farm and Food Society in London, in October 1983, A. H. Walters pointed out some of the problems associated with the over-use of artificial fertilizers,[3] and in February 1984 the Pesticides Action Network brought out a report of a recent inquiry into current agricultural practices in this country. This inquiry revealed that, in the United Kingdom, not only has the acreage which is sprayed with biocides risen steadily over the past several years, but that the number of times crops are sprayed per growing season has also increased.[4] The Ministry of Agriculture has estimated that in 1979 only 1 per cent of all vegetables grown in this country for human consumption *escaped* pesticide sprays, and that over half the pesticides applied to wheat comes through into the average loaf of bread.

Furthermore, over the same period, a number of articles have appeared in the medical and scientific literature, demonstrating the importance of diet in disease causation and prevention. Wheat, milk, eggs and oranges are the foods most commonly implicated in food sensitivities, and much has also been published on the role of food additives – artificial colourings, flavourings and preservatives – in the learning-disability syndrome and in behavioural disorders from depression to delinquency.[5,6,7]

Another point which has recently been stressed is the difficulty, if not the inadvisability, of prescribing a special diet for one family member, the patient, in isolation from his family. One individual, whether child or adult, suddenly required to eat differently from his family, will feel deprived, and possibly ostracized. Not only is it supportive to the patient if the rest of the family alter their diet, but the other family members often obtain an unexpected bonus in the form of improved health, since it is unlikely that it is only the patient who is being affected by the family eating pattern. He or she may simply be that member of the family who experiences the greatest problems.

The recipes in this book are all optionally wheat-free, and most of them are also dairy-food and egg-free. The recipes are therefore flexible and one recipe can be easily adapted to the needs of the whole family with just a little forethought as to when to add which ingredients.

In view of the recent support for our dietary ideas, and the increasingly widespread awareness of the importance of truly healthy eating, we feel that this book has a valuable part to play in the translation of theoretical dietary ideas into practical benefits on the dining table.

THE MACROBIOTIC APPROACH

Anyone who cares to follow the guidelines given so far will probably enhance his or her health. However, still further dimensions of diet can be explored, and an even more dynamic state of health and well-being can be achieved, through practising what has been termed the macrobiotic way of life.

It is always encouraging to find that someone supports your views on a subject, and very tempting then to imagine that you must both be right. In giving or receiving dietary advice, the effectiveness or otherwise of the prescription is quickly experienced, and few people will continue a method of eating in which they have little faith or understanding, or which fails to benefit them. Macrobiotics, sometimes defined as the 'great study of life', outlines a simple method of restoring balance and order to our lives.

In the past, its greatest exponents have come from the East (George Ohsawa and Michio Kushi), but macrobiotic philosophy has its counterpart in every culture, and as a result applies to us all, whatever our race, colour or creed.

Many people come to nutrition with the view that some foods are good and that others are bad. However, the ancient Taoist symbol for balance implies that the opposites, far from being separate, are very much involved in one another, interdependent and complementary. The terms yin and yang have been used to describe these opposite tendencies, and can be useful in explaining and establishing the best way of eating for specific individuals, according to their particular constitution and body type, and to give general guidelines for a healthier lifestyle.

This attention to detail may, at first, seem unnecessarily complicated, but in reality it is simply a way of putting into practice what our ancestors and many present inhabitants of this globe practise as a matter of course.

The modern western method of eating also exhibits a kind of balance, but without a main staple to give it a stabilizing centre point. The results are erratic eating, with ill-health exhibited by a vast majority of people.

Looking at a food chart classified according to yin and yang, it is tempting to imagine that one could balance meat eating with alcohol consumption, or eggs with sugar (as in a cake). In reality, however, these foods are too extreme examples of yin (expansion) and yang (contraction) and tend to set up a series of cravings for first one extreme and then the other. If you wish to reduce your alcohol consumption, increase your intake of wholegrains, pulses, nuts, seeds and vegetables, avoiding the expansive yin foods such as sugars, fruit drinks and vinegar, and avoid or reduce your intake of the contractive yang foods such as meats, salt, eggs, cheese and milk.

A simpler experiment is to eat less salt and experience less thirst.

Using the same chart it is easy to understand why someone who has become ill through eating a diet based on animal foods and salt will benefit temporarily from a swing to the opposite end of the scale, taking raw foods and juices. Similarly, the overweight person who has gained weight through eating sweets, biscuits and cakes,

YIN-YANG FOOD CHART

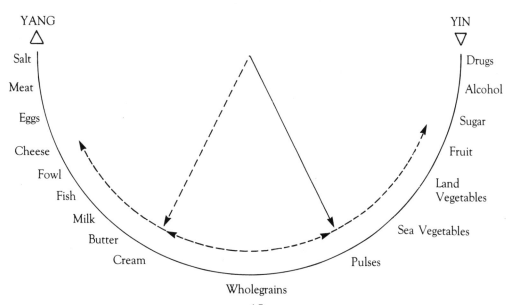

will achieve a temporary balance and weight loss by swinging to a high animal protein, low-starch, low-sugar diet.

It should be obvious, however, that any benefits gained in this way must inevitably be short-lived since such diets are in themselves unbalanced. They may correct the balance, but will not be able to maintain it. This is one of the main reasons why conventional dietary advice is limited in its effectiveness.

Mental and physical well-being, or good health, is more easily achieved, in our opinion, by eating a diet based on the staples of whole grains and pulses, supplemented by local, seasonal, fresh foods of both animal and vegetable origin, as are found to be individually suitable.

'You are what you eat . . .
    maybe that's why you feel so ill!'

Whatever we eat must be processed by our bodies, and either transformed, i.e. into our blood cells, bones, nerve tissue or other organs, stored or excreted. As we constantly break down and build up new cells and cell components, we gradually become a product of our food. It makes sense, therefore, to ensure that our food is the most suitable for the sort of person we wish to be. Wholesome or unhealthy, the choice, to a great extent, is ours.

In Cordon Bleu cookery, instructions are given to be followed to the letter. The recipes in this book allow for great flexibility of individual needs and desires, and have been included as much for their inspirational value as for their nutrient content.

The authors suspect that many of their readers are, like themselves, cookery book remodellers. No sooner do we start to read a recipe than we begin to alter it, cutting down on some ingredients, increasing the amounts of others, omitting some, including some, generally according to the ingredients available rather than what is advised in the text.

There are many cookbooks for ravenous omnivores and voracious vegetarians. This book is designed to show that eating for health can be economical and appealing to all the senses. We hope that it makes good sense to those who read, create and consume its contents.

The fact that you have bought, or are contemplating buying, this book indicates that you are one of a growing number of people showing an interest in wholesome nutrition, that is, food which looks good, tastes good and offers your body what it needs for good health. The food we eat plays a vital role in health maintenance and restoration and in disease prevention, and is part of a growing awareness of the responsibility we all have for our own health management.

The delicious recipes and menu suggestions which follow have been collected and devised to enable you to take the first steps towards attaining a more healthy and balanced way of life. All of the recipes can be made wheat-free and many of them are based on the yin/yang principle of macrobiotics. They taste good and generally appeal to the consumer of all ages. They are relatively inexpensive and make use of seasonal ingredients and basic staples.

'Eat, drink and be merry . . .
    for tomorrow you'll understand why!'

Bon appetit!

REFERENCES

1. Barlow, K., *The Law and the Loaf*, Precision Press, 1978.
2. Horrobin, D. F., 'Essential fatty acids: a review' in *Clinical Uses of Essential Fatty Acids* edited by D. F. Horrobin, Eden Press, Montreal, 1982.
3. Walters, A. H., 'Nitrate and cancer – a broader view' *The Ecologist*, 14, 32-37, 1984.

4. 'Pesticides, the case of an industry out of control.' Pesticide Action Network report, 1984.

5. Egger, J., Carter, C. M., Wilson, J., Turner, M. W. and Soothill, J. F., 'Is migraine food allergy? A double-blind controlled trial of oligoantigenic diet treatment.' *The Lancet, ii*, 865-869, 1983.

6. Egger, J., Carter, C. M., Graham, P. J., Gimby, D. and Soothill, J. F., 'Controlled trial of oligoantigenic treatment in the hyperkinetic syndrome.' *The Lancet, i*, 540-545, 1985.

7. Schauss, A. G., *Diet, Crime and Delinquency*, Parker House, 1981.

Porridges and Breakfast Recipes

Breakfast, at one time regarded as the most important meal of the day, has in recent years been relegated to the status of a quick snack or in some cases omitted altogether from the day's eating plan.

Not everyone can face the idea of cooking, or eating cooked food, first thing in the morning. This often results from imbalanced eating the previous day or night. The best way to work up an appetite for breakfast is to be an early riser and to avoid eating for at least three hours before going to bed. Taking a note of one's eating and drinking pattern for a few days often results in an awareness of the need for a change. It is very easy to develop less than healthy eating habits.

Selecting the right combination of foods can be important for ease of digestion. The foods eaten also depend on the season of the year.

The following ideas for seasonal breakfasts allow plenty of scope for individual variation.

In *Winter* choose from:

1. Porridge made from the following: oat flakes, barley flakes, rye flakes, whole oats, whole barley, brown rice or millet.
Choose one or more grains for a varied taste and texture.
Porridges can be served alone, or sprinkled with the following: toasted sunflower seeds, sesame seeds, pumpkin seeds, hazelnuts, almonds or walnuts.
Roasted, crushed seaweeds can be used in place of salt, and nuts and seeds can be toasted and then tossed in tamari/shoyu soya sauce.
A little soaked dried fruit can be used in combination with wholegrains, if well tolerated.
2. Homemade scones (p. 109), mixed grain breads (p. 104), oatcakes (p. 115) or crisp-breads, spread with low-sugar jams (p. 100), honey or savoury spreads such as seed or nut butters (p. 34), bean spreads (p. 32) or vegetable spreads (p. 34).
3. Vegetable juice or a mild, warming miso soup (p. 23).
4. Dried fruit salad served hot with muesli

In *Summer* choose from a wider range of fresh foods:

1. Muesli (p. 20).
2. Porridges made from brown rice or millet.
3. Corn bread.
4. Fresh seasonal fruit such as strawberries, peaches, pears, etc. topped with natural yogurt and toasted almonds or finely ground sunflower seeds.
5. Unsweetened fruit juice.

Suitable after-breakfast drinks include: wholegrain cereal 'coffees', roasted dandelion root 'coffee', mild, low tannin teas such as Japanese twig tea, and herb teas such as linden or lime flower.

All drinks are best taken without milk or sugar.

Grains need to be well chewed to release their flavour, and to aid their proper digestion, so try to resist the temptation to add liquids or to drink along with a grain dish.

PORRIDGE RECIPES

A wide selection of porridges can be made from the following flaked grains: barley, brown rice, buckwheat, maize, millet, oats, rye, wheat. It is recommended that you use grains which have been organically grown (see page 13 in the Introduction).

QUICK PORRIDGE

3 oz (85g) oat flakes
Pinch of sea salt
12 fl oz (340ml) water

1. Soak the oats in half the water overnight.

2. In the morning, add a further 6 fl oz (170ml) water, and cook gently over a medium heat, stirring occasionally to prevent burning and the formation of lumps.

3. Serve with or without milk, or with natural yogurt.

CREAMY OATS

2 oz (55g) whole oats
¾ pint (425ml) water
2 oz (55g) oat flakes
Pinch of sea salt

1. Bring the whole oats to the boil in the water, turn off the heat and leave in the covered pot overnight.

2. In the morning add the oatflakes and salt and a further ¼ pint (140ml) water, to make a creamy textured porridge cooked over a low heat, stirring occasionally.

3. Serve with toasted sunflower seeds or flaked almonds, soaked sultanas, or milk. Seeds have a sweet, nutty flavour which blends well with the grain.

BROWN RICE BREAKFAST DISH

¾ lb (340g) cooked brown rice (p. 37)
Pinch of sea salt
½ pint (280ml) water
Optional ingredients: 1 tablespoon toasted sesame or sunflower seeds, flaked almonds or hazelnuts,
1 tablespoon toasted and finely ground nuts or seeds,
2 teaspoons sunflower seed spread, peanut butter or sesame tahini,
4 oz (110g) carrot, finely grated,
1 tablespoon soaked sultanas, apricots or prunes,
½ an umeboshi plum (p. 84)

1. Combine the rice, salt and water in a pot and stir over a medium heat until the 'porridge' begins to thicken.

2. Add the nut or seed spread for a creamy texture and taste, or carrot to lighten the dish and give a refreshing, sweet flavour.

3. Serve the rice topped with toasted nuts or seeds, soaked dried fruit or finely chopped umeboshi plum.

Note: As with all grain dishes, eat slowly and chew well.

A similar dish may be made using a combination of grains such as brown rice and barley, brown rice and oats or brown rice and millet.

Muesli Porridge

4 oz (110g) wheat-free muesli base
½ pint (280ml) water
Pinch of sea salt
Milk or natural yogurt (optional)

1. Pre-soak the muesli in water overnight.

2. In the morning add the salt and a little more water, if required.

3. Put into a pot and cook over a gentle heat for 15-20 minutes to thicken.

Note: Avoid muesli which contains sugar or honey.

Summer Muesli
(Serves 1)

1 level tablespoonful organic oatflakes
3 tablespoons water
1 tablespoon freshly squeezed lemon juice
1 tablespoon unsweetened natural yogurt, or almond or sesame seed purée, or soya milk
½ lb (225g) sweet, ripe apples
1 tablespoon freshly ground, lightly toasted hazelnuts, almonds or sunflower seeds

1. Soak the oatflakes in the water overnight.

2. In the morning add the lemon juice and yogurt.

3. Coarsely grate the apples, and stir at once into the oats.

4. Serve garnished with the nuts and seeds.

Note: For those prone to indigestion, it is recommended that you chew your food thoroughly and that all sweeteners (sugar, honey, dried fruit, etc.) be omitted from this dish.

Wheat-free Muesli Base

3 tablespoons each of oatflakes and barley flakes
1 tablespoon each of brown rice flakes, millet flakes and rye flakes
1 tablespoon sunflower seeds (plain or lightly toasted)
1 tablespoon raisins or sultanas
1 tablespoon flaked nuts (hazelnuts, almonds, cashews or walnuts)

1. Combine all the ingredients, mix well and store in an airtight jar.

2. Cook as a porridge or soak 1 tablespoonful per person overnight in a little water.
In the morning mix with unsweetened apple juice or natural yogurt to serve.

Soups and Starters

Soup is a traditional dish, designed to warm and nourish whilst making the best use of limited cooking facilities and ingredients. Soups can be substantial in texture and rich in flavour, almost a meal in themselves, or delicately flavoured like a bouillon stock, to encourage the appetite for the meal to follow.

The outer leaves of vegetables, well scrubbed roots and stalks, and sea vegetables supply valuable nutrients to a basic soup stock. The liquid from cooked pulses and unseasoned, steamed, boiled or blanched vegetables should also be saved and added to the soup pot. Vegetables cooked in the minimum of water, or steamed, retain more of their flavour and nutrients but what is removed is not lost if the cooking water is added to the next pot of soup. Leaving seasoning until the end of cooking will lessen the need for salt as you develop a taste for the subtle flavours of fresh foods. Babies and young children should not be given salty food, and adults would also benefit from using less. The occasional use of herbs adds variety and enjoyment and can also aid digestion.

Clear summer soups can be made using onion, carrot, sea vegetables, puréed pumpkin, cauliflower, etc., in a miso broth (p. 23).

More filling winter broths can be made with freshly prepared or left-over pulses and grains used along with seasonal vegetables, sea vegetables and miso or yeast extract. These ingredients can be combined to produce a wonderful variety of nourishing but quickly and easily made soups.

Health From The Sea

The cultivation of *seaweeds*, nourishing and tasty sea vegetables, has been carried out in Japan since the 1700s in its shallow coastal waters. Coastal communities throughout the world have recognized the worth of this food source but sadly only a few still use seaweeds in their daily diet, or realize their value. The mineral and trace element composition of sea water, and of the plants that grow in it, is similar to that of human blood. The sea vegetables are therefore an ideal source of the minerals and trace elements required by the body.

The flavour and texture of sea vegetables are varied and they become increasingly appealing with use. They are *the* most economical vitamin and mineral supplement on the market and have the advantage of containing their nutrients in natural proportions, unlike commercially produced vitamins and mineral pills. They are available in dried form from health and wholefood shops, or freshly harvested from uninhabited rocky shorelines. Dried sea vegetables expand considerably when re-hydrated and cooked, so that a little goes a long way.

The sea vegetables most readily available at present include kombu, wakame, arame and nori, which come from Japan, dulse, carrageen and agar-agar from Ireland and Britanny, and sugar ware, finger ware, dabberlocks, grockle, dulse and sea lettuce (nori) from Scotland.

Miso, a fermented soya bean paste, is an excellent source of protein, vitamins, minerals and trace elements, as well as being an excellent seasoning and flavouring agent for soups, casseroles, stews, gravies, sauces, spreads and dips. It has been used for centuries in Japan and is produced by a long fermentation process, resulting in enzymic breakdown of the soya bean proteins to readily assimilable amino acids. It encourages the growth of beneficial bacteria in the intestinal tract and provides enzymes which aid digestion. During the fermentation process vitamin B_{12} is produced, making miso one of the rare non-animal sources of this vitamin.

Tamari and shoyu are soya sauces prepared by long fermentation. Shoyu contains some wheat but tamari is wheat-free.

Growing children, the elderly, invalids, those living in towns and cities or the increasingly mechanized countryside, pregnant and nursing mothers, and those with stressful occupations, will especially benefit from the use of sea vegetables, sea-vegetable stock and miso in their soups.

VEGETABLE STOCK

**2 pints (1.1 litres) water or stock from cooked vegetables
1-2 teaspoons yeast extract (p. 84)**

1. Heat the water or stock and use to dissolve the yeast extract.

2. Use this instant stock to flavour soups, casseroles, gravies and sauces.

KOMBU STOCK

**2 pints (1.1 litres) water
One 6 inch (15cm) strip of kombu seaweed**

1. Bring the water to the boil with the kombu, and simmer for 20-30 minutes.

2. Use the resulting stock for soups, casseroles, gravies and sauces. Slice the kombu into strips and add to stews or casseroles.

KOMBU AND GINGER BROTH

This broth is ideal for those with head colds and poor appetites.

**One 6 inch (15cm) strip of kombu seaweed
6oz (170g) onion, finely sliced
2 pints (1.1 litres) water
6oz (170g) carrot, cut into carrot flowers or matchsticks (p. 138)
1-2 tablespoons spring onion, finely sliced
1-2 tablespoons tamari/shoyu soya sauce
1 inch (2.5cm) piece of fresh ginger root, peeled and grated**

1. Simmer the kombu and onion in the water for 15 minutes, then add the carrot.

2. Simmer for a further 15 minutes, then remove the kombu, slice finely and return to the pot.

3. Remove the soup from the heat, add the spring onion, and shoyu to taste.

4. Finally squeeze in the juice from the grated ginger root.

MISO BROTH

Miso is available as a paste, or in a powdered form. An instant soup is easily made by adding water, which is just off the boil, and stirring. Some powdered varieties contain onion and seaweed, and make a quick and tasty soup which is ideal for travelling, for quick lunches and for mid-morning or mid-afternoon breaks. It can also be used as a light breakfast.

Miso makes a tasty and nourishing flavouring agent for soups and stews. To make a soup using wakame or arame seaweeds, with or without seasonal vegetables, simmer the seaweeds until tender, remove a little of the hot broth to dissolve the miso paste (use ¼-½ teaspoon miso per person, or for each ½ pint [280ml] bowl of soup), add the miso to the soup pot, and simmer for 3-5 minutes to blend the flavours. Do *not* boil as this would inactivate the beneficial enzymes in the miso.

The basic recipe can be made more interesting and attractive by serving with a suitable garnish (p. 78).

TYPES OF MISO

Hatcho miso, made from soya beans and sea salt: a strong salty miso not suitable for children.
Mugi miso, made from soya beans, sea salt and barley: a rich flavoured miso for winter use.
Genmai miso, made from soya beans, sea salt and brown rice: a lighter miso for summer use.
Kome miso, made from soya beans, sea salt and white rice.
Instant miso soup powder, available plain or with seaweed.

The following recipes serve 4-6 people. Larger quantities may be made by increasing the total ingredients, or by diluting the soup with extra water and adjusting the flavour. To save on time spent in the kitchen, it makes sense to prepare sufficient soup to last 2-3 days. For the best flavour, dilute and season just prior to use.

Onions used in soups and other savoury dishes can either be sautéed in a little oil or simmered.

SCANDINAVIAN SUMMER SOUP OR FIRST CROP SOUP

½ lb (225g) mild young onions or spring onion bulbs
2 pints (1.1 litres) kombu stock (p. 22)
½ lb (225g) fresh pea pods
½ lb (225g) new potatoes
½ lb (225g) new carrots, chopped
½ lb (225g) cauliflower sprigs
1-2 teaspoons miso or yeast extract
½ fresh lemon, finely sliced
2-3 sprigs watercress

1. Dice the onions and par-cook in one-quarter of the stock, then add the peas, potatoes, carrots and cauliflower.

2. Add the remainder of the stock, cover with a tightly fitting lid and simmer until just tender, approximately 3-5 minutes.

3. Flavour lightly with miso, and serve with lemon slices and watercress sprigs.

SUMMER SOUP

½ lb (225g) onions, sliced
2 pints (1.1 litres) vegetable stock (p. 22)
1 lb (455g) sweetcorn kernels
4 oz (110g) bean sprouts (mung, aduki, etc.)

1. Simmer the onion in one cup of stock until tender.

2. Add the sweetcorn and the remaining stock, cover and simmer for 20 minutes.

3. Serve garnished with beansprouts.

CORN CHOWDER

½ lb (225g) white fish – haddock,
whiting, etc. (optional)
4 fl oz (110ml) tamari/shoyu soya sauce
10 oz (280g) onions, finely sliced
1 lb (455g) sweetcorn kernels
½ lb (225g) carrots, sliced
1 bayleaf
Pinch of dried or fresh thyme
2 pints (1.1 litres) water
4 oz (110g) tofu or natural yogurt
(optional)
2-3 spring onions, finely sliced

1. Marinate the fish in the soya sauce for 2
hours.

2. Simmer the onions, sweetcorn, carrots
and herbs in the water for 15 minutes.

3. Add the fish and simmer for a further 10
minutes.

4. Remove the bay leaf, then sieve or
liquidize and gently reheat.

5. Add the tofu or yogurt, if used, taste and
adjust the seasoning.

6. Serve garnished with the spring onions.

COUNTRY VEGETABLE SOUP

One 6 inch (15cm) strip of kombu
seaweed
1 lb (455g) onions, sliced
½ lb (225g) carrots, diced
½ lb (225g) broccoli, cut into florets
½ lb (225g) cauliflower, cut into florets
2 pints (1.1 litres) water
1-2 teaspoons miso or yeast extract

1. Place the kombu on the base of the pot,
then top with the onion, carrot, broccoli and
cauliflower.

2. Add the water, cover, bring to the boil,
and simmer for about 20 minutes until the
vegetables are tender.

3. Blend the miso in a little of the hot soup,
add to the pot, and simmer for a few
minutes, to blend the flavours.

4. Remove the kombu, slice into fine strips
and serve with the soup.

CELERIAC OR CELERY SOUP

¾ lb (340g) onions, finely sliced
1 tablespoon vegetable oil (optional)
Pinch of sea salt
½ lb (225g) carrots, diced
1 bay leaf
1 lb (455g) celeriac or celery, sliced
2 pints (1.1 litres) water
1 tablespoon fennel leaves

1. Gently sauté or simmer the onions with a
pinch of salt, until tender.

2. Add the carrot, bay leaf, celeriac and
water.

3. Simmer for about 20 minutes, until the
vegetables are tender. Remove the bay leaf.

4. Sieve or liquidize the soup, taste and
adjust the seasoning as required.

5. Reheat and serve garnished with finely
chopped fennel leaves.

CABBAGE SOUP

½ lb (225g) onions, sliced
Pinch of sea salt
1 tablespoon vegetable oil (optional)
½ lb (225g) potatoes, sliced
1 lb (455g) cabbage, finely sliced
2 pints (1.1 litres) water
1-2 teaspoons yeast extract
Pinch of nutmeg (optional)
2 tablespoons spring onions, finely
chopped

1. Sauté or simmer the onion with the salt until tender.

2. Stir in the potato and then the cabbage and cook for 5-10 minutes, stirring occasionally.

3. Add the water and yeast extract, bring to the boil and simmer for 30 minutes.

4. Before serving, add the nutmeg and garnish with the spring onions.

CAULIFLOWER SOUP

1 tablespoon vegetable oil
½ lb (225g) onions, sliced
Pinch of sea salt
1 lb (455g) cauliflower, cut into sprigs
½ lb (225g) leeks, sliced (optional)
2 pints (1.1 litres) water or kombu stock
(p. 22)
1-2 teaspoons miso or yeast extract
Croûtons, to garnish

1. Heat the oil, if using, and sauté or simmer the onion with the salt, until tender.

2. Add the cauliflower, leek and water, bring to the boil, and simmer until the vegetables are just cooked.

3. Sieve, or liquidize, reheat, taste and season as liked with miso or yeast extract.

4. Serve garnished with small cubes of toasted cheese or herb croûtons (p. 79).

MUSHROOM CONSOMMÉ

½ lb (225g) onions, sliced
1-2 teaspoons oil (optional)
1 lb (455g) mushrooms
2 pints (1.1 litres) water or kombu stock
(p. 22)
1 bay leaf (optional)
1-2 teaspoons miso or tamari/shoyu
soya sauce
Spring onions, chives or parsley

1. Sauté or simmer the onion and cook until golden but not brown.

2. Add the mushrooms and cook for a further 3 minutes, then add the water and bay leaf and simmer until mushrooms are tender.

3. Strain off the stock (keeping the vegetables to use in another dish – ideal for bean loaves and stir-fries).

4. Season the soup to taste with miso and serve garnished with finely chopped spring onions, chives or parsley.

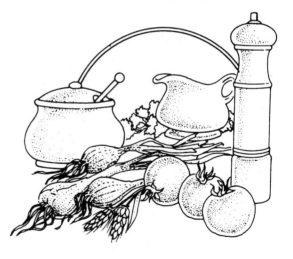

CARROT SOUP

½ lb (225g) leeks or onions, finely sliced
2 teaspoons oil (optional)
Pinch of sea salt
1 lb (455g) carrots, sliced
4 oz (110g) whole green or brown lentils,
washed
½ teaspoon dried thyme
2 pints (1.1 litres) water or kombu stock
(p. 22)
4 oz (110g) cooked brown rice (p. 37)
optional
½ fresh lemon, finely sliced

1. Sauté or simmer the leek with salt until
tender.

2. Add the carrots, lentils, thyme and water,
bring to the boil and simmer for 30 minutes.

3. Sieve or liquidize the soup with the
brown rice.

4. Reheat, taste and adjust the seasoning if
required and serve garnished with lemon
slices.

CREAM OF CARROT SOUP

1 lb (455g) carrots, diced
4 oz (110g) onion, diced
2 pints (1.1 litres) water or kombu stock
(p. 22)
4 oz (110g) cooked brown rice (p. 37)
1-2 teaspoons miso or yeast extract

1. Simmer the carrot and onion in water
until tender.

2. Sieve or liquidize with the rice, reheat and
adjust the seasoning to taste with miso or
yeast extract.

3. Serve garnished with finely chopped fresh
parsley or chives, a swirl of natural yogurt or
herb-tossed Croûtons (p. 79).

AUTUMN HARVEST SOUP

1-2 teaspoons oil
½ lb (225g) onions, finely sliced
Pinch of sea salt
½ lb (225g) pumpkin, diced
½ lb (225g) carrots, diced
½ lb (225g) sweetcorn kernels
2 pints (1.1 litres) water
1-2 teaspoons miso or yeast extract
1-2 tablespoons parsley or spring onions

1. Warm a large, heavy soup pot and brush
with the oil. Add the onion and salt, and
sauté until transparent, stirring to prevent
burning.

2. Stir in the remaining vegetables and cook
for 3 minutes before adding the water.
Simmer gently for 30 minutes, until the
vegetables are tender.

3. Leave the vegetables whole, or sieve or
liquidize. Reheat and season with the miso
and serve garnished with the parsley or
spring onions.

PUMPKIN SOUP

½ lb (225g) onions, diced
1-2 tablespoons oil (optional)
1 lb (455g) pumpkin, diced
2 pints (1.1 litres) water or kombu stock
(p. 22)
1-2 teaspoons miso or yeast extract

1. Simmer or sauté the onion for 5 minutes.

2. Add the pumpkin and the water and
simmer for 15-20 minutes until tender.

3. Season to taste with the miso and simmer
for a further 3 minutes to blend the flavours.

4. Serve garnished with fresh, chopped
herbs.

Pumpkin Purée Soup

¾ lb (340g) onions, finely sliced
1 tablespoon oil (optional)
Pinch of sea salt
1 lb (455g) pumpkin
6 oz (170g) carrots, sliced
2 pints (1.1 litres) water
1-2 teaspoons miso or yeast extract

1. Sauté or simmer the onion with the salt until transparent.

2. Remove the rind from the pumpkin and slice into 1 inch (2.5cm) cubes. Add to the pot with the carrots, cover with the lid and allow to cook gently for 3-4 minutes.

3. Add the water and simmer for 20-30 minutes until the vegetables are tender.

4. Sieve or liquidize, then reheat, taste and season as required.

5. Serve garnished with freshly chopped parsley, spring onions or chives. This soup has a warm, golden colour, rich flavour and smooth, velvety texture.

Oatmeal and Onion Soup

½ lb (225g) onions, diced
½ lb (225g) carrots, diced
1 stick celery, sliced
2 pints (1.1 litres) water or kombu stock (p. 22)
1-2 teaspoons miso or yeast extract
4 oz (110g) fine oatmeal
2 inch (5cm) strip of dried dulse seaweed

1. Place the vegetables in a heavy pot with half the water and the seasoning.

2. Cover and simmer gently until the vegetables are tender.

3. In a separate pot heat the remaining water and gradually stir in the oatmeal, to ensure an even consistency. Cook for 10 minutes to thicken before adding to the soup pot.

4. Mix well, taste and adjust seasoning before serving, garnished with dulse seaweed which has been rinsed to rehydrate, and then finely sliced.

Super Soup

2 pints (1.1 litres) water
½ lb (225g) onions, finely sliced
½ lb (225g) carrots, diced
2 oz (55g) mushrooms, sliced
2 stalks celery, diagonally sliced
½ lb (225g) green beans, fresh peas or sweetcorn kernels
½-1 teaspoon sea salt, miso or yeast extract
3 oz (85g) cooked barley or brown rice (p. 37), optional

1. Heat the water, then add and simmer the onions for 10 minutes, before adding the remaining vegetables and the seasoning.

2. Simmer for a further 15 minutes, then add the cooked grain and heat through before serving.

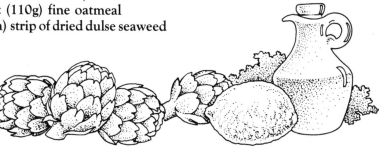

LENTIL SOUP WITH SPROUTS

½ lb (225g) onions, sliced
2 pints (1.1 litres) vegetable stock
flavoured with yeast extract
½ lb (225g) potatoes, diced
1 bay leaf
4 oz (110g) cooked lentils (p. 37)
4 oz (110g) sprouted lentils (p. 140)

1. Simmer the onion in half the stock until tender.

2. Add the potatoes, bay leaf and remaining stock and simmer for 15 minutes.

3. Remove bay leaf then sieve or liquidize with the cooked lentils.

4. Reheat and serve garnished with the lentil sprouts.

MUSHROOM BROTH

½ lb (225g) onions, finely sliced
1 clove garlic, finely sliced (optional)
Pinch of sea salt
2 pints (1.1 litres) water or kombu stock
(p. 00)
½ lb (225g) fresh mushrooms or 3½ oz
(100g) dried shitake mushrooms*
4 oz (110g) barley, dry roasted
4 oz (110g) cooked black-eyed beans
(p. 37)
2 inch (5cm) piece of fresh root ginger,
peeled and grated (optional)
1 tablespoon tamari/shoyu soya sauce or
1 teaspoon yeast extract

1. Simmer the onion and garlic with the salt in ½ pint (280ml) water or stock until 'frothing' disappears.

2. Add the mushrooms, barley and remaining water or stock, bring to the boil, cover and simmer for 30-40 minutes until the barley is cooked.

3. Stir in the beans, ginger juice (squeezed from the grated fresh ginger) and soya sauce, and allow the flavours to blend before serving.

*If using dried mushrooms, pre-soak for 15 minutes, discarding the stalks.

LENTIL AND VEGETABLE SOUP

½ lb (225g) onions, diced
½ lb (225g) mixed vegetables – carrot,
turnip, parsnip – diced
2 pints (1.1 litres) water
½ lb (225g) cooked whole green or
brown lentils (p. 37)
1 teaspoon miso or yeast extract
Watercress sprigs and white or cottage
cheese, to garnish

1. Simmer the vegetables in the water for 15 minutes until tender.

2. Add the lentils, taste and adjust the seasoning.

3. Serve the soup sprinkled with sprigs of watercress and finely grated white cheese or a low-fat cottage cheese.

LENTIL SOUP WITH KOMBU CRISPS

4 oz (110g) barley
2 oz (55g) lentils
6 inch (15cm) strip of kombu seaweed
½ lb (225g) onions, diced
2 pints (1.1 litre) water
1 stalk celery, sliced
½ lb (225g) carrots, diced
Pinch of sea salt or 1 tablespoon tamari/
shoyu soya sauce

1. Rinse the barley and the lentils.

2. Place the kombu on the bottom of a heavy soup pot and cover with the onion, barley, lentils and water.

3. Cover and bring to the boil then reduce the heat and simmer for 40 minutes

4. After 20 minutes add the remaining vegetables and the seasoning. Remove the kombu, slice into 1 inch (2½cm) strips and gently crisp in a low oven or under the grill.

5. Serve garnished with the kombu crisps.

RICH LENTIL OR SPLIT PEA SOUP

½lb (225g) lentils or split peas, rinsed, soaked and drained
3 pints (1.7 litres) water or kombu stock (p. 22)
Pinch of dried oregano, thyme and a bay leaf (optional)
½lb (225g) onions, finely sliced
½lb (225g) carrots, diced
2 stalks celery, sliced
2-3 teaspoons miso or yeast extract
2 oz (55g) natural yogurt or tofu
1 tablespoon parsley, freshly chopped

1. Combine the lentils with the water and the dried herbs. Bring to the boil and simmer for 30 minutes, until tender.

2. Add the vegetables and cook for a further 15 minutes.

3. Remove the bay leaf, sieve or liquidize, reheat and flavour to taste.

4. Serve with a spoonful of yogurt and the parsley.

BEAN AND CABBAGE SOUP

3 oz (85g) onion, sliced
1 clove garlic, finely sliced (optional)
1 tablespoon oil (optional)
2 pints (1.1 litres) water or vegetable stock
½lb (225g) red or white cabbage, shredded
4 oz (110g) barley
Pinch of thyme or basil
½lb (225g) skinned tomatoes (optional)
½lb (225g) cooked kidney beans (p. 37)
1-2 teaspoons miso or yeast extract
2 inch (5cm) cube of fresh ginger root, grated (optional)
2 tablespoons natural yogurt or tofu (optional)

1. Sauté or simmer the onion and garlic for 5 minutes.

2. Add the water, cabbage, barley, herbs and tomatoes, and simmer for 30 minutes.

3. Add the beans and season to taste, including the ginger juice if liked.

4. Simmer gently for 5 minutes to blend the flavours and serve with a swirl of yogurt.

MEAL IN A BOWL SOUP

½lb (225g) onions, sliced
1 clove garlic, sliced
Pinch of sea salt
3 pints (1.7 litres) water
1 large leek, finely sliced
½lb (225g) carrots, diced
6oz (170g) courgettes or turnip, sliced
6oz (170g) Brussels sprouts or
cauliflower, sliced
Pinch of basil, oregano or thyme
(optional)
½lb (225g) cooked beans of choice
(p. 37)
4oz (110g) cooked brown rice (p. 37)
1-2 teaspoons miso or yeast extract

1. Simmer the onion, garlic and salt in half
the water for 10-15 minutes.

2. Add the remaining vegetables, herbs and
water and simmer gently for 20-30 minutes
until the vegetables are tender.

3. Stir in the pre-cooked beans and rice, and
heat through.

4. Taste and adjust the seasoning. Store in
the refrigerator for use over the following 3-
4 days. This recipe is ideal for a snack lunch.

CREAMY OAT AND DULSE SOUP

This is a delicious, rich-flavoured soup, ideal
for cold winter evenings.

2oz (55g) oat flakes
2 teaspoons oil
½lb (225g) onions, finely sliced
Pinch of sea salt
½lb (225g) carrots, diced
2 pints (1.1 litres) water or vegetable
stock
2 teaspoons tamari/shoyu soya sauce or
yeast extract
½ cup dulse seaweed, finely shredded

1. Dry toast the oat flakes in a heavy pot over
a medium heat, stirring constantly, until
golden. Remove from the pot and set aside.

2. Heat the oil in the pan and add the onion
and the pinch of salt. Cook gently without
the lid for 3-5 minutes.

3. Add the carrots, cover and cook for a
further 5 minutes.

4. Add the stock and the oats, cover and
cook over a low heat until the vegetables
and the oats are cooked.

5. Sieve or liquidize the soup, reheat, taste
and adjust the seasoning. Serve garnished
with the dulse.

Menu suggestion:
Creamy oatmeal and dulse soup
Bean and onion stew
Steamed Chinese leaves
Millet balls with spring onions and pickled
cabbage.

DULSE SOUP

1 cup dried dulse
2 pints (1.1 litres) water
½ lb (225g) onions, sliced
Pinch of sea salt
1 tablespoon oil (optional)
2 oz (55g) porridge oats

1. Rinse the dulse thoroughly, shred and add to the water in the soup pot.

2. Sauté or simmer the onion with the salt until tender. Add the oats and stir for a further minute before adding to the soup.

3. Bring to the boil and simmer for 30 minutes. Taste and adjust the seasoning as required.

ARAME SOUP

1 cup dried arame seaweed
½ lb (225g) onions, finely sliced
2 pints (1.1 litres) water
6 oz (170g) carrots, diced
1-2 teaspoons miso or 1-2 tablespoons tamari/shoyu soya sauce

1. Soak the arame in a bowl of water for 3 minutes, then rinse well to remove any sand or grit.

2. Meanwhile simmer the onion in half the water for 10 minutes, add the carrot, arame and remaining water, and simmer for a further 20 minutes.

3. Dissolve the miso in a little hot broth and add to the soup. Leave for 2-3 minutes for the flavours to blend before serving.

MEDITERRANEAN FISH SOUP

2 teaspoons oil
½ lb (225g) onions, finely sliced
Pinch of sea salt
2 sticks celery, sliced
2-3 tomatoes (optional)
1 clove garlic, sliced
A generous pinch each of fresh or dried basil, oregano and green anise
2 bay leaves
2 teaspoons ground coriander
1 pint (570ml) water or kombu stock (p. 22)
1 lb (455g) whiting or haddock
4 oz (110g) shrimps or prawns
2 oz (55g) hard white cheese, cottage cheese or tofu

1. Heat the oil and gently sauté the onions with the salt for 4-5 minutes in a large soup pot.

2. Add the celery, tomatoes, garlic and other herbs and sauté for a further 4-5 minutes to soften the vegetables and blend the flavours.

3. Add the water and fish and simmer gently until the fish is cooked. Remove the bay leaves and sieve or liquidize the soup.

4. Return the soup to the pot, reheat and finally stir in the shrimps (overcooking makes them tough).

5. Serve sprinkled with a little white cheese or with a swirl of soft cottage cheese or tofu.

DEEP SEA CHOWDER

½ lb (225g) onions, finely sliced
4 sticks celery, sliced
1 small red or green pepper, de-seeded
and sliced
6 oz (170g) potatoes, sliced
1 lb (455g) sweetcorn kernels
1 tablespoon oil
Pinch of sea salt
Pinch of dill seed, fennel seed, marjoram,
savory, sage and/or thyme
½ pint (280ml) fish stock (made from
the simmered bones and skin of the fish)
1½ pints (855ml) water or kombu stock
(p. 22)
1½ lb (680g) white fish – cod, haddock
or whiting
4 oz (110g) shrimps
1 tablespoon arrowroot or kuzu
(optional)

1. Sauté the vegetables in the oil with the
salt and herbs for 5 minutes, stirring
occasionally.

2. Add the stock and water and simmer for
15 minutes.

3. Cut the fish into cubes, add to the pan
and cook gently until tender.

4. Add the shrimps, taste the soup and
adjust the seasoning as required.

5. Dissolve the arrowroot or kuzu in a little
cold water and stir into the soup to thicken.

LENTIL PÂTÉ

1-2 teaspoons oil
1 small onion, finely sliced
Pinch of sea salt
½ lb (225g) mushrooms, finely sliced
(optional – if omitting, use extra onion)
½ lb (225g) cooked lentils (p. 37)
1-2 tablespoons tahini
1-2 teaspoons miso or yeast extract
2 tablespoons chopped parsley
Stock from the cooked lentils to moisten
mixture, if required

1. Heat the oil and lightly sauté or shallow
fry the onion with a pinch of salt, then add
the mushrooms.

2. Combine all the ingredients and stir until
the texture is thick and smooth.

3. Turn the mixture into a bowl and allow to
cool.

4. Serve on toast or crispbread, as a sandwich
spread or formed into rissoles as a salad
ingredient.

Note: Use whole brown lentils for a result
which resembles liver pâté.
Finely grated carrot can also be added. If
desired, the top can be sprinkled with
sesame seeds.
Half to one cup of sunflower seed meal,
made by toasting and grinding the seeds,
makes a nourishing and tasty addition.

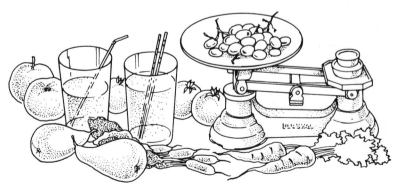

Mushroom Pâté or Spread

¾ lb (340g) onions, very finely sliced
1 clove garlic, crushed
1 tablespoon oil
Pinch of sea salt
1 lb (455g) mushrooms, sliced
Small pinch of freshly grated nutmeg
4 slices mixed grain bread, crispbread or
puffed brown rice cakes (p. 130)

1. Lightly sauté the onion and garlic in the oil with the salt.

2. Add the mushrooms and, when tender, the nutmeg.

3. Remove from the heat, cool, sieve or liquidize and serve with toast and salad.

Chick Pea Spread

This spread can be used as: a sandwich filling, toast topper or party starter when served on toast circles on a bed of finely shredded crisp lettuce and sliced radishes. To use as a dip, add puréed cooked carrot, vegetable or bean stock to dilute to a dip consistency. Serve with crudités, e.g. carrot sticks, celery stalks, tiny spring onions, blanched cauliflower sprigs, etc.
Lentils and beans can also be used to make similar tasty spreads.

½ lb (225g) cooked chick peas (p. 37)
4 tablespoons tahini sesame cream
2 tablespoons finely chopped spring
onions or 1 lightly sautéed onion
1-2 teaspoons tamari/shoyu soya sauce
or yeast extract
Juice of ½ lemon (add to taste)
1 tablespoon freshly chopped parsley

1. Drain the chick peas and reserve the stock.

2. Finely blend or mash the chick peas, and combine with the tahini, onion and seasoning.

3. Add the lemon juice according to taste, and mix in the parsley.

Super Spread

This mixture makes a good substitute for butter or margarine. It has half the cholesterol content of the same weight of pure butter, and avoids the artificial processing required to produce commercial margarine.

½ lb (225g) fresh or lightly salted butter
8 fl oz (225ml) good quality cold-pressed
vegetable oil, e.g. safflower, sunflower,
corn or sesame oils

1. Cut the butter into small chunks and cream by hand or in a food mixer or blender.

2. Mix in the oil gradually, a few drops at a time and continue beating until a light, creamy, smooth consistency is obtained.

3. Transfer to a bowl or tub, cover, and refrigerate until firm.

NUT BUTTER

Undiluted nut butters are too high in oil for easy digestion, but blended as follows they make a tasty and nutritious spread.

8 fl oz (225 ml) water
1 onion, finely diced
1 teaspoon miso or yeast extract
4 tablespoons tahini or nut butter
(choose those makes which contain nuts and sea salt only, or blend your own using lightly toasted nuts or seeds)
1 tablespoon parsley, finely chopped

1. Heat the water, add the onion and simmer for 5 minutes.

2. Blend the miso with a little of the hot liquid, add to the pot, but do *not* allow to boil.

3. Stir in the tahini or nut butter and the parsley and cook, stirring occasionally, until the mixture thickens to a spreadable texture. It will stiffen further as it cools.

4. Use at once, or keep in a screwtop jar in the refrigerator.

ONION SPREAD

2 lb (900g) onions, finely sliced
1 tablespoon oil
Pinch of sea salt
1-2 tablespoons water

1. Gently sauté the onions in the oil with a pinch of sea salt for 2-3 minutes.

2. Add the water, and cook slowly, stirring occasionally, until the mixture is smooth and very sweet.

3. Cool, cover and store in jam jars in the refrigerator. Use within 7 days.

CARROT SPREAD

2 lb (900g) carrots, chopped
1-2 tablespoons water
1 tablespoon miso or yeast extract

1. Simmer the carrots gently in the water until tender.

2. Sieve or blend and simmer again with the miso. Stir frequently and cook without lid to thicken.

3. Cool, cover and store in jam jars in the refrigerator. Use within 7 days.

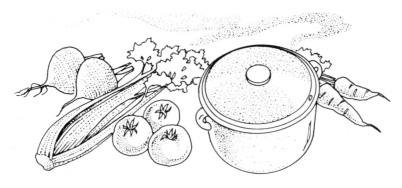

Main Meals
and Vegetables

In this book we have not included recipes for meat or poultry dishes as there is no lack of these. We have concentrated on recipes for the lesser known foods – wholegrains, pulses, and sea vegetables, as well as some recipes for fish. However, if you are using meat and poultry, always choose genuine free-range produce. Impossible to find? Then create a demand, and try not to eat intensively reared or factory-farmed meats, fish, poultry, eggs or dairy produce. Wholegrains and pulses (peas, beans and lentils, also known as legumes) can be combined in innumerable ways to make inexpensive, appetizing, satisfying and nourishing meals. Always use organically grown produce where possible.

Refined cereals such as white rice, semolina, white cornflour, etc., are lacking in the essential nutrients, fibre and flavour provided by their wholegrain equivalents (brown rice, organically grown whole wheat, maize meal etc.), making refined foods poor value in terms of cost and nourishment.

Vegetable stock or kombu seaweed stock may be used in place of water in all savoury recipes, soups, stews, casseroles and sauces. Kombu stock is a particularly rich source of calcium and other minerals and trace elements. (N.B. Do *not* stir grains or beans during cooking.) Use heavy pots with tightly fitting lids. This shortens cooking time and uses less water. Pressure cookers can be used successfully for whole grains and the larger beans but not for the smaller beans.

Wholegrains can be cooked on their own, seasoned simply with a pinch of sea salt. Alternatively, sauté an onion in 1-2 teaspoons cold-pressed sunflower, sesame or corn oil, with a pinch of sea salt until just tender; then add grain and stir to toast for 3-5 minutes before adding the water or vegetable stock.

OR cook as above but add diced carrot, sliced celery, spring onions etc., before adding the grain.

OR cook as above, but add ½ teaspoon dried herbs such as thyme, marjoram, oregano, mixed herbs, parsley etc., to the cooking water.

Saffron rice is a colourful salad ingredient. Simply add a *pinch* of saffron herb (literally one grain) to the cooking water.

Other grains can be combined with brown rice such as,

rice and barley
rice and whole oats
rice and millet,

while toasted seeds or ground or chopped toasted nuts added to cooked grain gives a nutritious blend of flavours, e.g.,

pre-cooked chestnuts	sunflower seeds
sesame seeds	pumpkin seeds
almonds	hazelnuts
walnuts	pecans.

Adding 1-2 tablespoons soaked raisins or sultanas to the above recipe gives a Middle Eastern flavour.

Grains can be served with vegetable sauces – sieve or blend thick vegetable soup, thicken with kuzu or arrowroot, and season with tamari/shoyu soya sauce.

Left-over grain can be added to soups, mixed with pulses to make a 'loaf' or steamed savoury pudding, served cold with a salad, or formed into balls or patties with vegetables, pulses, egg and/or cheese (optional) to make grill burgers, shallow fry patties, deep fried rissoles or oven casseroles.

Combining grains and beans will make the protein they contain more available for our use. In general use between 2 and 4 parts cooked grain to 1 part cooked pulses.

Pulses (peas, beans and lentils) are best cooked with seaweed, which provides the minerals and trace elements so necessary for their proper digestion. They are best seasoned at the end of cooking, otherwise they will toughen and take longer to cook.

Always wash and rinse grains and pulses well, removing dust, husks, small stones and twigs.

Most pulses require pre-soaking, which will cut down cooking time. Soak in fresh cold water, and stand in a cool place for 6-24 hours or overnight. Lentils can be used without pre-soaking. Taste and digestibility are improved by cooking with a piece of kombu seaweed. In all recipes using pulses, this can be removed after 30 minutes, and either added to a pot of water to make a soup stock, or dried gently in a low oven, crushed to a powder and mixed with roasted, crushed sesame seeds to make a mineral-rich table seasoning for brown rice and vegetable dishes.

Pulse stock (the liquid remaining after the pulses are cooked) is a useful source of B group vitamins and minerals such as calcium, and can be used to flavour soups, sauces and casseroles. For variety, add vegetable chunks to the pulse pot during the last 20 minutes of cooking. The standard kombu and pulse stock, flavoured with tamari/shoyu soya sauce, can be varied by seasoning with sea salt or yeast extract instead, and adding sliced onions, garlic or herbs, such as bay leaf (lovely with lentils), basil, sage, oregano, thyme or bouquet garni during cooking.

Some grain and bean mixtures also cook well together from the dry state, e.g.,

brown rice and aduki beans

barley and brown lentils

brown rice and brown lentils.

Buckwheat is not a grain but a member of the dock and rhubarb family. It is, however, referred to as a grain because of its similar usage. Originating in China, Russia and northern India, it was introduced into Europe during the Middle Ages by the Crusaders and was cultivated in northern Europe and England for several centuries. Its ability to grow on poor soil, its good quality protein and its high content of B and E vitamins have made buckwheat an excellent, nutritious food, especially in cold, damp climates.

Buckwheat flour is sometimes used to make bread and beer, but is more often used in pancakes, biscuits and as buckwheat noodles (also called soba). When baked, it has a rich, agreeable taste.

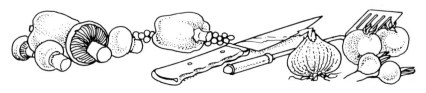

COOKING TIMES FOR GRAINS

1 cup dry grain	cups water	cooking time in minutes
pot barley	2½-3	40-60
whole oats	2½-3	40-60
brown rice, short grain	2	40
brown rice, long grain	2	30
millet	3	35
buckwheat	3	25
whole rye grains	3	120
corn or maize meal (polenta)	4	25-30
oat, barley and rye flakes	3-4	10-20 pre-soaking lessens cooking time
basmati rice	2	10-15

STANDARD RECIPE FOR GRAINS

Put the measured dry grain into a cooking pot, fill with cold water, swirl to separate the husks, dust, etc., from the grain, and pour off the water. Repeat twice. Add the measured quantity of water and sea salt (¼ teaspoon to 1-2 cups of dry grain). Cover, bring to the boil and simmer until all the water is absorbed. Do not stir during cooking.

COOKING TIMES FOR PULSES

1 cup dry pulses	cups water – simmering time		cups water – pressure cooking	
aduki beans	3-4	1½-2 hours	not such a suitable method	
chick peas (garbanzos)	3-4	3 hours	3	1 hour
brown and green lentils	3-4	1 hour	3	20 minutes
black and red kidney beans	4	1½-2 hours	4	40 minutes
black-eyed beans	3	1½ hours	3	35 minutes
pinto beans, broad and butter beans, scarlet runner beans	3	1½ hours	3	1 hour
split peas	3	1 hour	3	40 minutes
soya beans, black & white			4	3 hours or more
tofu (high protein, low fat soya bean curd)	add to stir-fries or casseroles and cook gently for 5-20 minutes, depending on the type of dish.			

STANDARD RECIPE FOR PULSES

All pulses, except lentils and split peas, require pre-soaking. Soaking times vary with the type of bean, i.e. from 3 hours for aduki beans to overnight for kidney beans. Always boil pulses for at least 10 minutes before reducing the heat to complete cooking. If using a slow cooker, remember to boil the pulses first to inactivate a substance found in them which inhibits protein digestion.

Rinse the soaked beans, put a 6 inch (15cm) piece of kombu seaweed in the bottom of a heavy pot (this helps to prevent burning) and add the beans and the measured amount of water. Cover, bring to the boil, boil for 10 minutes and simmer for the appropriate time. Season to taste at the end of cooking with sea salt or shoyu/tamari, for a rich but not too salty flavour.

When cooking grains and pulses, 2 cups of dried beans will serve approximately 6 people, and 2 cups of dried grain will serve approximately 4 people.

COOKING VEGETABLES

Steaming is one of the best cooking methods for vegetables, preventing loss of the water-soluble B group vitamins and vitamin C. The longer the cooking, the greater the vitamin loss. Vegetables look and taste best undercooked rather than overcooked, and the cooking liquid can be used to make a sauce. Thicken with arrowroot or kuzu, flavour with tamari and ginger juice or yeast extract and serve with the vegetables.

Cooking makes some vegetables more digestible, but will not improve the flavour or appearance of those which are not fresh or are of poor quality. Never soak vegetables in water. Instead, wash quickly prior to use.

Lightly boiled, steamed or sautéed vegetables can make a meal in themselves, or colourful and tasty accompaniments for main-course dishes. There are occasions when the vegetable can make all the difference between a plain grain/pulse dish and an attractive and appetizing meal. Recipes such as Glazed Onion Chrysanthemums and Walnuts (p. 39) and Wakame and Carrots (p. 42) suggest how this may be accomplished.

Most of the recipes in this section will feed 4-6 people, depending on the appetites of the consumers.

THICKENERS

When making gravies and sauces, refined cornflour is the most readily available thickener. However, many other less refined alternatives are available, and are often preferable for use by those with food sensitivities. For those who are over-weight, it is best to avoid thickened foods.

Recommended alternatives include:
arrowroot — prepared from the root of a water plant,
kuzu — prepared from the root of a Japanese mountain vine,
brown rice flour,
barley, rye or organically-grown whole-wheat flour,
oatmeal,
potato flour,
buckwheat flour,
chick pea flour,
soya flour.

GLAZED ONION CHRYSANTHEMUMS AND WALNUTS

8 small onions
½ teaspoon sea salt
1½ pints (840ml) water
1 teaspoon miso or yeast extract
1-2 tablespoons kuzu or arrowroot,
dissolved in a little cold water
4 oz (110g) chopped, toasted walnuts

1. Cut two slices, at right angles to each other, two-thirds of the way through each small onion. Rotate the onion and cut another slice half way through two quarters, and repeat for the remaining diagonal. (See p. 139.)

2. Boil the onions with a little sea salt in the cooking water, until tender, cooking them in batches to prevent overcooking.

3. Drain and cool on a wire rack, then place in a shallow ovenproof casserole.

4. Use the onion stock seasoned to taste and thickened with kuzu or arrowroot, to make the glaze. Form the chrysanthemums by pushing down the onion petals with the fingers. Pour the glaze over them and sprinkle with the chopped, toasted walnuts.

5. Serve hot or cold.

SUNFLOWER SEED AND ALMOND ROAST

1 tablespoon oil (optional)
1 large onion, finely chopped
1 green pepper, diced (optional)
1 clove garlic
¼ pint (140ml) stock or water
1 teaspoon miso or yeast extract
6 oz (170g) ground sunflower seeds
6 oz (170g) ground almonds
4 oz (110g) rye breadcrumbs or oat flakes
½ teaspoon oregano
½ teaspoon sage
Pinch of sea salt

1. Heat the oil, if using, and sauté or simmer the onion, pepper and garlic until tender.

2. Add the stock and stir in the miso.

3. Add the remaining ingredients, with a little extra water if necessary, to make a moist mixture.

4. Line a 2 lb (900g) loaf tin with greaseproof paper. Pour in the mixture and bake for 45 minutes at 375°F/190°C/gas mark 5.

BROCCOLI AND WALNUTS

**¾lb (340g) broccoli
1 small bunch of spring onions
Pinch of sea salt or 1 teaspoon tamari/
shoyu soya sauce
2oz (55g) coarse-cut walnuts**

1. Lightly steam the broccoli.

2. Sauté the spring onions with the salt or tamari/shoyu for 3-4 minutes.

3. Add the coarse-cut walnuts, mix with the broccoli and serve at once.

BRUSSELS SPROUTS AND CHESTNUTS

**½lb (225g) dried chestnuts
Water
Pinch of sea salt**

1. Soak the chestnuts overnight.

2. Cook in boiling salted water in a covered pot for 1 hour, or until tender.

3. Drain and cut into eighths.

4. Mix with the sprouts as above, or sauté first and season with tamari.

Variations:
Other good vegetable and nut mixtures include the following: blanched celery, toasted almond flakes and freshly chopped parsley; baked onions and pecans; cashew nuts and asparagus.

BRUSSELS SPROUTS AND ALMONDS

**1oz (28g) flaked, blanched almonds
¾lb (340g) Brussels sprouts**

1. Sauté the blanched almonds in a little sunflower oil, or simply dry toast.

2. Lightly boil the Brussels sprouts and serve mixed with the almonds.

Note: Alternatively, walnuts may be used instead of almonds.

CAULIFLOWER WITH SUNFLOWER SEEDS

**1 large cauliflower
6oz (170g) sunflower seeds
Tamari/shoyu soya sauce to taste**

1. Cut the cauliflower into florets, keeping the outer leaves for soup, and steam until tender.

2. Toast the sunflower seeds in a dry pan over a low heat, or under the grill. Sprinkle with the shoyu sauce mixed with a little water and stir.

3. Serve the cauliflower sprinkled with the seeds on a bed of cooked brown rice or millet.

CAULIFLOWER CRUSTY

4 oz (110g) cooked brown rice (p. 37)
4 oz (110g) mixed grain or rye bread crumbs
4 oz (110g) sunflower seeds
1 sautéed onion
1 teaspoon mixed herbs
¼ pint (140ml) water
1 large cauliflower
2 tablespoons tamari/shoyu soya sauce or 1 teaspoon yeast extract
1 tablespoon arrowroot or kuzu
4 oz (110g) flaked toasted almonds or hazelnuts

1. Combine the first 5 ingredients, and press into a shallow ovenproof dish. Bake for 15 minutes in a hot oven.

2. Bring the water to the boil in a heavy pot with a tightly fitting lid. Add the cauliflower, sectioned into 6 pieces, and cook for 8-10 minutes, until just tender.

3. Drain the cooking liquid into a saucepan and add the tamari to taste.

4. Dissolve the arrowroot or kuzu in a little cold water and add to the cauliflower stock, made up to ½ pint (280ml). Bring to simmering point and stir until the mixture forms a clear sauce.

5. Arrange the cauliflower on top of the crusty base and cover with the sauce. Bake at 425°F/220°C/gas mark 7 for 15-20 minutes.

6. Serve garnished with chopped parsley or sliced spring onions, and the toasted, flaked nuts. Serve hot or cold.

Note: The sauce can also be made using vegetable or bean stock and rye or barley flour.

STEAMED CAULIFLOWER AND SUPER SAUCE

2 large onions, finely chopped
Pinch of sea salt
1 tablespoon oil
4 oz (110g) mushrooms
Sweetcorn from 1 fresh cob
2 medium carrots, finely grated
1 inch (2.5cm) fresh ginger, grated and squeezed to remove the juice
1 large cauliflower
1 tablespoon flaked nuts or seeds, toasted

1. Sauté the onions with the salt in the oil until soft, then add the mushrooms, the sweetcorn and finally the carrot.

2. Add the ginger juice, cover and allow to sweat for 10-15 minutes.

3. Lightly cook the cauliflower, drain off any liquid and reserve.

4. Drain off any liquid from the sautéed vegetables, add to the cauliflower liquid and make up to ½ pint (280ml) with water, checking the seasoning (add shoyu or tamari rather than more salt). Thicken with soya flour or arrowroot and add the sautéed vegetables.

5. Serve the cauliflower covered with the vegetable sauce, and garnished with toasted, flaked nuts or seeds.

WAKAME AND CARROTS

**2 oz (55g) wakame seaweed
½ pint (285ml) water
¾ lb carrots, diced
1-2 tablespoons tamari/shoyu soya sauce
1 dessertspoon arrowroot/kuzu dissolved
in 2 dessertspoons water**

1. Soak the wakame for 5 minutes in the water.

2. Chop the wakame and add, with the soaking water, to the carrots. Bring to the boil and simmer for 15 minutes until the carrots are just cooked.

3. Remove the vegetables, flavour the stock with the tamari/shoyu and thicken with the arrowroot.

4. Pour the sauce over the vegetables and serve either hot or cold.

CABBAGE AND GINGER

**1 small white cabbage
1 umeboshi plum
⅛ pint (70ml) water
1 inch (2.5cm) fresh root ginger
2 teaspoons arrowroot or kuzu for
thickening**

1. Quarter the cabbage then slice into shreds. Place in a covered pot with the umeboshi plum and water and cook until tender.

2. Drain the stock into a small pot, add the juice from the grated ginger, and thicken with the arrowroot or kuzu, dissolved in a little water.

Note: Arrowroot comes from the root of a water plant and kuzu comes from the root of a land plant. It is more alkaline than arrowroot and has medicinal properties which recommend its use for those with weak or upset digestive systems.
Try the same recipe with cauliflower.

BAKED PUMPKIN WITH PARSNIPS AND CARROTS

**1½ lb (670g) pumpkin, cut into 2 inch
(5cm) cubes
1 lb (455g) carrots, cut into matchsticks
½ lb (225g) parsnips, cut into matchsticks
3 teaspoons oil
1 dessertspoon honey (optional, this is a
naturally sweet dish)
1 teaspoon sea salt
A little freshly ground black pepper
(optional)**

1. Sauté the vegetables lightly in the oil for 5-10 minutes.

2. Add the honey and seasoning, then bake in a covered, ovenproof casserole for 30-40 minutes, at 375°F/190°C/gas mark 5.

3. Serve garnished with freshly chopped parsley.

SCALLOPED POTATOES

**1 lb (455g) potatoes
2 onions
½ lb (225g) carrots
4 oz (110g) green beans
½ lb (225g) cooked green lentils (p. 37)
Water, bean or vegetable stock
Grated cheese, nuts or breadcrumbs for
topping**

1. Slice potatoes and onion very thinly and slice the carrots and green beans.

2. Layer the vegetables and the lentils in a casserole, barely cover with the water or stock, cover and cook for about an hour at 325°F/170°C/gas mark 3.

3. When cooked, uncover and sprinkle with the cheese, nuts or breadcrumbs, and cook for about 10-15 minutes to brown.

BAKED POTATOES

These make inexpensive, filling, tasty and nourishing snack meals. There is a wide choice of toppings, examples of which are listed below.

½ lb (225g) potato per person
1 tablespoon oil or butter (optional)

1. Pre-heat the oven to 400°F/200°C/gas mark 6.

2. Scrub the potatoes clean and remove any blemishes.

3. Make a cross cut into the top half of each potato. If liked, rub the surface lightly with oil and place in an ovenproof dish.

4. Bake for 1 hour until the inside is tender and the outside is crisp.

5. Place each potato on the serving dish, widen the slit and add the topping of choice. Alternatively, halve the potatoes, scoop out the potato, blend with the filling, return to the potato shell and re-heat in the oven or under the grill.

Toppings:
● 1 tablespoon natural yogurt or cottage cheese, mixed with freshly chopped parsley, chives or other fresh herbs, or a pinch of paprika.
● 1 tablespoon cottage cheese with 1 oz (28g) finely grated white Cheddar cheese and ½ tablespoon freshly chopped spring onion and finely grated carrot.
● 1 oz (28g) Feta cheese (sheep or goat's milk) and 1 tablespoon diced cucumber.
● 1 tablespoon cooked lentils or beans – for instance, left-overs from hot pots and casseroles.
● 1 tablespoon shallow-fried vegetables – onion, mushrooms, beansprouts, celery, etc.
● 1 tablespoon vegetable sauce (see Cauliflower Sauce, p. 91), sautéed onion, red pepper, tomato purée, mixed herbs, tamari/shoyu soya sauce.

● ½ hard boiled egg, mixed with 1 tablespoon natural yogurt and 1 teaspoon finely chopped chives.

STIR-FRY VEGETABLES

Stir-fry is one of the quickest ways of cooking vegetables with the minimum of nutrient loss and the tastiest result. The idea is to use the least amount of oil possible. Use a pastry brush to coat lightly the surface of the heated pan or wok. The oil acts as a super-efficient heat conductor which greatly reduces the cooking time and makes a true stir-fry suitable even for low-fat cookery.

All the vegetables for stir-fry should be finely and evenly cut. If stir-frying a selection of vegetables, start as always with the onions, then the root vegetables such as carrot sticks or slices, slope-cut celery stalks, blanched broccoli or cauliflower florets, finely shredded cabbage, then the watery and leafy vegetables – Chinese leaves, cucumber, watercress and beansprouts.

A mixture of vegetables, varying the colour, texture and taste, is very successful.

BATTERED VEGETABLES WITH GINGER DRESSING

All deep-fried foods are recommended for occasional use only. To help balance oily dishes, serve with a delicate ginger/shoyu dressing.
Have all ingredients to hand before you start and make the batter immediately before use.

Ginger Dressing:
**3 inches (7.5cm) fresh ginger root, finely grated
1 cup water
1 cup tamari/shoyu soya sauce**

Batter:
**Safflower or sesame oil for deep frying
¾ lb (340g) barley flour
2 oz (55g) arrowroot flour
2 oz (55g) brown rice flour or maize meal
Pinch of sea salt
8 fl oz (225ml) cold water**

Vegetables:
**Turnip sticks
Carrot sticks
Cauliflower florets
Broccoli sprigs
Parsley sprigs
Watercress
Onion rings**

1. Squeeze the juice from the grated ginger into a small bowl. Mix well with the water and the tamari/shoyu to make the dressing and set aside.

2. Heat the oven to 250°F/130°C/gas mark ½ to keep the fried vegetables warm between batches. Have two baking trays prepared with sheets of draining paper.

3. Heat the oil to 350°F/180°C. A mixture of 90 per cent safflower oil and 10 per cent sesame oil is good for both flavour and heat conduction. Test with a spoonful of batter dropped into the oil. It will fall and rise slowly when the temperature is right.

4. Mix the ingredients into a thick batter, using more or less water as required. Avoid overstirring.

5. Arrange a selection of vegetables in order of cooking, choosing from the selection above and adding others as liked.

6. Dip the vegetables in the batter to coat, but allow to drain off the excess before dropping into the heated oil.

7. Cook the vegetables in batches to prevent temperature drop and uneven cooking. Chopsticks are useful utensils for coating vegetables in batter, and for dipping the deep-fried vegetables in the ginger dip.

8. Serve with long grain brown rice, blanched watercress, finely diced spring onions, radishes or sauerkraut, steamed leafy green vegetables and herb-flavoured beans.

ORIENTAL ARAME AND CABBAGE

**1 cup dry arame
1 medium onion, finely sliced
1 tablespoon oil
½ small head of cabbage, finely shredded
1 inch (2.5cm) piece of fresh ginger
1 tablespoon tamari/shoyu soya sauce**

1. Soak the arame in fresh cold water for 15 minutes and then wash well to remove any sand.

2. Remove the arame and carefully pour off one cup of the soaking liquid, taking care not to pour out any sand or grit. Reserve this liquid.

3. Sauté the onion in the oil until soft, stir in the arame, the cabbage and the arame water, and simmer for 15 minutes.

4. Stir in the juice of the freshly grated ginger and the tamari, cover, and simmer gently for 5-8 minutes, until the flavours have blended. The gravy may be thickened if desired. (See p. 89 for Arrowroot Sauce.)

BAKED VEGETABLE FILLER

Stuffed marrows, pumpkins, peppers, etc. make colourful party dishes. Create your own favourite filling based on the following recipe. It is particularly good with a crunchy side salad of celery, spring onions, watercress, radish, cabbage, etc.

½ lb (225g) cooked beans or lentils (p. 37)
4 oz (110g) cooked grain – millet, brown
rice or buckwheat (p. 37)
½ onion, diced
1 tablespoon miso or yeast extract,
diluted in 2 fl oz (55ml) bean stock
1 teaspoon fresh mustard (optional)
2 oz (55g) sunflower seeds, toasted

1. Pre-heat the oven to 350°F/180°C/gas mark 4.

2. Combine the beans, grains, onion, miso and mustard.

3. Parboil the vegetable to be stuffed, i.e. whole, de-seeded, red, green or yellow peppers, rings of vegetable marrow, or sliced pumpkin, for 5 minutes in lightly salted water.

4. Drain, lightly brush the outsides with oil and place in a lightly oiled ovenproof dish. Fill with the mixture and bake uncovered for 20 minutes.

5. Serve hot on a bed of long-grain brown rice, or fluffy cooked millet, sprinkled with sunflower seeds.

STUFFED CABBAGE

1 medium savoy or primo cabbage

Stuffing:
1 tablespoon oil
1 medium onion
Pinch of sea salt
½ teaspoon mixed herbs
4 oz (110g) carrot, finely diced or grated
½ lb (225g) buckwheat, precooked (p. 37)
4 fl oz (110ml) vegetable or bean stock

Glaze:
¾ pint (420ml) arrowroot/kuzu sauce (p. 89)

1. Divide the cabbage into leaves, then wash and boil or steam in batches until tender. Drain and cool.

2. Prepare the stuffing. Heat the oil and sauté the onion with the salt and the herbs, for 5 minutes.

3. Add the carrot and buckwheat and heat through.

4. Stir in the well-flavoured vegetable or bean stock to make a stiff paste, and allow to cool.

5. Cut the centre stalk from the larger cabbage leaves. Place ½-1 tablespoon of the stuffing in the centre of each leaf and roll up, tucking in the sides and ends to form a neat parcel.

6. Place the rolls in rows in a shallow ovenproof serving dish, cover with the glaze, and heat through in the oven at 350°F/180°C/gas mark 4. Can be served hot or cold.

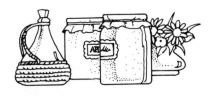

ORIENTAL SUCCOTASH

An adaptation of a traditional American Indian recipe for butter (lima) beans and sweetcorn.

1 tablespoon oil
½lb (225g) onions, sliced
½lb (225g) cooked, fresh sweetcorn kernels (cook in boiling water until just tender, on or off the cob)
4oz (110g) cooked beans (p. 37) unseasoned
1 teaspoon miso or yeast extract
Pinch of paprika (optional)
2oz (55g) white cheese
1-2 tomatoes (optional)
1 tablespoon chopped parsley or spring onions

1. Heat the oil in a heavy pot, add the onion, corn and beans, and sauté over a low heat for 5 minutes.

2. Dilute the miso in a little bean stock, add the paprika, and stir into the mixture in the pot.

3. Place in an ovenproof casserole topped with the finely grated white cheese and sliced tomato.

4. Toast under the grill and serve sprinkled with the chopped parsley.

SWEETCORN CASSEROLE

In season, July to September, fresh sweetcorn adds a delicious light but rich flavour wherever it is used.

6oz (170g) cooked, drained beans (p. 37)
¾lb (340g) sweetcorn kernels
1 teaspoon miso or yeast extract
1 onion, finely sliced
1 carrot, diced
8fl oz (225ml) bean stock
2oz (55g) toasted sunflower or sesame seeds, or breadcrumbs

1. Preheat the oven to 350°F/180°C/gas mark 4.

2. Mix all the ingredients except the seeds or breadcrumbs and put into a lightly oiled casserole.

3. Bake, covered, for 30-40 minutes.

4. Uncover and sprinkle with the toasted seeds or breadcrumbs and bake for a further 10 minutes.

5. Serve hot with plain boiled rice and a seasonal salad, or use cold as a lunch-box filler.

WINTER VEGETABLE PIE

1lb (455g) potatoes
2 onions
2 leeks
Pinch of sea salt
2 teaspoons oil (optional)
6oz (170g) carrots, diced
4oz (110g) turnip, diced
½ pint (280ml) stock
1 teaspoon miso or yeast extract
2oz (55g) hazelnuts, flaked
2oz (55g) sunflower seeds

1. Boil and then mash the potatoes.

2. Sauté or simmer the onions and the leeks with a pinch of sea salt until soft, stir in the carrots and turnip, add the stock and simmer for 5-10 minutes.

3. Season with miso or yeast extract.

4. Place the vegetables in a casserole, top with the potato and sprinkle with the nuts and seeds. Bake for ½ hour at 350°F/180°C/gas mark 4.

VEGETABLE STEW

This recipe has the best flavour when made several hours before being eaten. It is ideal for reheating.

1 tablespoon oil
3 medium onions, cut in eighths
2 medium carrots, cut diagonally into 1 inch (2.5cm) chunks
6 oz (170g) thinly sliced rounds of daikon/mooli radish
¾ lb (340g) potatoes, sliced
10 oz (280g) sliced cabbage – white, savoy or Chinese
¾ pint (420ml) water or kombu stock
1 bay leaf (optional)
1-2 teaspoons miso or yeast extract
2 tablespoons freshly chopped fresh herbs

1. Heat the pot and brush with oil.

2. Add the onions, then the carrots, daikon, potatoes and cabbage, one at a time, sautéing each for about 2 minutes.

3. Add the water and bring to the boil. (If wished, omit the oil and simmer the vegetables instead of sautéing.)

4. Reduce the heat, add the bay leaf, cover and simmer for 15-20 minutes.

5. Add the miso blended in a little hot stock and simmer for a further 3-5 minutes.

6. Serve garnished with the fresh herbs.

Note: For extra nourishment, add ¾ lb (340g) cooked beans or cubes of tofu (soya bean curd) before adding the water. The basic recipe can be varied using any combination of seasonal vegetables and by the addition of sea vegetables.

ONION FLAN

Pastry:
3 oz (85g) rye or barley flour
3 oz (85g) oat flakes
Pinch of sea salt
3 oz (85g) Super Spread (see p. 33) or oil
2-4 tablespoons ice-cold water

Filling:
¾ lb (340g) onions
2 teaspoons oil
½ teaspoon sea salt
¼ teaspoon mixed herbs

1. To make the pastry, mix the flour and oats with the salt, rub in the Super Spread and add sufficient ice-cold water to give a workable consistency.

2. Roll the pastry out and use to line a greased pie dish.

3. Slice the onions finely and sauté gently in the oil with the salt and herbs until transparent.

4. Turn into the pie dish and bake for 30-40 minutes at 350°F/180°C/gas mark 4 until cooked.

Note: You can vary this basic recipe by using alternative fillings such as the following: onions and carrots; tomatoes and basil; mushrooms in sauce.

PUMPKIN PIE

This recipe can also be made using vegetable marrow and carrots instead of pumpkin.

1 teaspoon oil
2 large onions, very finely sliced (to give a sweet flavour when cooked)
3 lb (1.3 kg) pumpkin
Pinch of sea salt
⅓ pint (200ml) water
2 tablespoons dry roasted sesame seeds

For pie case:
½ lb (225g) whole rye, barley or organically grown whole wheat flour
½ teaspoon wheat-free baking powder (p. 103)
Pinch of sea salt
3 tablespoons oil
2-4 tablespoons cold water

1. Heat a heavy pan and brush with oil.

2. Sauté the onions until transparent.

3. Add the washed and cubed pumpkin, the salt and the water. Bring to the boil and simmer for 30 minutes, or until pulpy.

4. Mash, or purée with a blender or food mill, and allow to cool.

5. For the pastry: in a bowl, combine the flour, baking powder and salt.

6. Add the oil and rub the mixture to form 'breadcrumbs'.

7. Add the cold water gradually to form a stiff dough. Knead for approximately 8 minutes, until smooth. Then roll out on a floured board.

8. Line a pie dish with the pastry and fill with the pumpkin purée. Sprinkle with sesame seeds and bake for 30 minutes until golden brown (425°F/220°/gas mark 7).

SUNFLOWER BARLEY HOT POT

1 onion, chopped
1 teaspoon oil
2 stalks celery, finely chopped
¾ lb (340g) finely chopped mushrooms
1 tablespoon barley, organic whole wheat or soya flour
12 fl oz (340ml) vegetable stock
1 teaspoon yeast extract
½ teaspoon thyme
½ teaspoon basil
½ lb (225g) ground almonds
6 oz (170g) sprouted sunflower seeds
¾ lb (340g) barley, pre-cooked (p. 37)

1. Sauté the onion in the oil in a large pan, add the celery and the mushrooms, and cook over a gentle heat until soft.

2. Remove from the heat, sprinkle in the flour and stir until smooth.

3. Add the stock, yeast extract and herbs, and stir again until smooth and well blended.

4. Add the ground almonds, sunflower sprouts and barley.

5. Mix well to heat through and serve.

AUTUMN BARLEY STEW

A traditional British country dish.

1-2 teaspoons oil
2 large onions, finely sliced
½ teaspoon sea salt
1 medium carrot, diced
1 medium parsnip, diced
1 medium swede, diced
1 medium turnip, diced
1 strip of kombu, presoaked for 10 minutes
2 pints (1.1 litres) stock
½ lb (225g) pot barley
Sweetcorn from 1 cob
1-2 tablespoons tamari/shoyu soya sauce

1. Heat a heavy stewpan, coat with oil and sauté the onions with the salt until transparent.

2. Add the root vegetables and the kombu, cut into 1 inch (2.5cm) strips.

3. Cover with the stock and bring to the boil.

4. Add the barley which has been thoroughly washed and drained. Replace the lid and cook in a very low oven overnight, or over a very low heat for 3 hours. The barley may be placed in a muslin bag, loosely tied to allow for swelling of the grain. This prevents the stew from becoming mushy.

5. Add the sweetcorn kernels and the soya sauce 15 minutes before serving. Stir to mix and serve piping hot.

Wholegrain Casserole

6 oz (170g) rye grains, pot barley or whole oats
or 3 oz (85g) brown rice and 3 oz (85g) whole rye, pot barley or whole oats
16 fl oz (450ml) water
½ teaspoon sea salt
1 teaspoon oil
1 clove garlic (optional)
2 leeks, cut into 1 inch (2.5cm) slices
2 oz (55g) flaked hazelnuts or almonds, dry roasted

1. Wash and drain the wholegrains, and then roast in a heavy pot until they are dry and begin to crack. Stir constantly to prevent burning.

2. Add the water and salt, cover, and simmer for 45 minutes until all the water is absorbed and the grain has a nutty texture.

3. Heat the oil and sauté the garlic and leeks with a pinch of salt, then add the nuts and one tablespoon water. Cover and simmer gently for 20 minutes, until the leeks are tender.

4. Meanwhile, transfer the grain to an ovenproof casserole. Top with the vegetable mixture and place in a low oven at 300°F/150°C/gas mark 2, for 15 minutes to heat through.

5. Serve with boiled greens or a seasonal salad.

Chestnut Roast

2 large onions
4 sticks celery
1 tablespoon oil
1 lb (455g) shelled, cooked chestnuts or ½ lb (225g) cooked, dried chestnuts
½ lb (225g) cooked brown rice (p. 37)
1 free-range egg (optional) or 8 fl oz (225ml) vegetable stock
Sea salt to season, if required

1. Chop the onions and celery and sauté lightly in the oil.

2. Cover the pan and allow the vegetables to sweat for a further few minutes.

3. Chop or purée the chestnuts, depending on the texture desired, keeping a few whole for decoration.

4. Combine the chestnuts with the vegetables, stir in the cooked brown rice and add the egg or stock to bind. Adjust the seasoning, turn into a greased 9 inch (20cm) mould and bake or steam for 30-40 minutes at 350°F/180°C/gas mark 4.

RICE BALLS

These are one answer to the sandwich problem. (See p. 139.)

1 lb (455g) cooked short-grain brown rice (p. 00)
2-4 umeboshi plums (optional)
4 sheets nori seaweed

Rice balls are made using freshly cooked, or left over, brown rice, or brown rice and other cereal grain mixtures. Short-grain brown rice gives the best results as it is more sticky in texture.

When cooled, form the rice into compact balls, the size depending on preference, and the purpose for which they are intended; small rice balls make attractive party treats and travelling food, they look appetizing, and keep better. The tighter the ball, the better. Use hands which have been moistened in a little water or bancha twig tea, and with the hands at right angles to each other, rotate and squeeze the rice into the palm of the left hand (if right-handed). This will form a flat-topped circle. Triangular shapes can also be formed which will fit well into lunch boxes, and seem to keep longer! To increase the keeping qualities, and to enhance the taste, ½ teaspoon of paste made from umeboshi plums (p. 84) can be inserted into the centre of the ball. Simply bore a hole with a skewer, insert the plum, and remould.

Nori seaweed is obtainable in fine sheets which, when toasted on the rough side, can be quartered and used to wrap up the rice balls. For parties, serve these garnished with blanched carrot flowers, pickled cucumber triangles or parsley sprigs. To make the nori go further, cut into strips and use these to circle across the top of the rice ball. Garnish as above.

Diced, cooked vegetables can be mixed with the rice before forming into balls, but too much vegetable will make the rice difficult to handle. Rice balls make a nourishing and sustaining dish, ideal for picnics, packed lunches and hikers. Roasted nuts or seeds added to the rice provide extra flavour and nourishment.

SUSHI

This is an ideal way to serve rice for parties and picnics. (See p. 140.)
Summer sushi can be made by mixing the rice with 1-2 teaspoons of brown rice vinegar.

3 sheets nori seaweed
1 lb 2 oz (500g) cooked rice, made slightly moist and sticky
1½ teaspoons umeboshi paste

Choice of Fillings:
2 oz (55g) carrot sticks, blanched
1 bunch watercress, blanched
1 tablespoon sauerkraut or other pickle
3 small spring onions and 2 oz (55g) cucumber strips

1. Lightly toast the nori sheets on the rough side only, until the colour changes from dark to pale green. This takes only a few seconds.

2. Lay the nori sheets on a sushi mat, or square of greaseproof paper.

3. Dampen the hands and press the rice over the nori and flatten to an even thickness of ¼ inch (0.5cm). The rice needs to be softly cooked. Keep the rice in from the edges, especially the far-away edge. One-third of the way up, make a depression and line with ½ teaspoon umeboshi paste.

4. Press in the vegetables or pickles. Use the mat or the greaseproof paper to roll up the nori (like making a Swiss roll).

5. Squeeze the roll in the mat to firm. Cut into 1 inch (2.5cm) rounds to serve.

SESAME SEED AND RICE PARCELS

8-10 large cabbage leaves or Chinese leaves
10 oz (280g) brown rice, cooked (p. 37)
1 dessertspoon sesame seeds
1 teaspoon fennel or celery seeds
½ teaspoon oregano
1-2 dessertspoons tahini sesame cream (optional)
1 dessertspoon tamari/shoyu soya sauce

1. Steam the greens gently until tender.

2. Mix the rice with the rest of the ingredients and spoon on to the leaves.

3. Wrap up each leaf and place in an ovenproof dish, with the folds downwards so that they do not unwrap. Dot with butter or vegetable oil.

4. Cover and bake for 20 minutes at 350°F/180°C/gas mark 4.

BAKED SAVOURY RICE

This recipe can also be made using whole barley, oats, buckwheat or millet, adjusting the amount of water required, depending on the grain (see table, p. 37).

½ lb (225g) short-grain brown rice
½ tablespoon oil
2 large onions, thickly sliced
1-2 cloves garlic, chopped (optional)
Pinch of sea salt
4 medium carrots cut in chunks
10 inch (25cm) piece of daikon/mooli radish cut in thick diagonal slices
½ small cabbage or 2 turnips, sliced
2 pints (1.1 litres) boiling water or vegetable stock

1. Dry roast the rice in a large, heavy ovenproof cooking pot, until lightly browned. Remove to a bowl.

2. Add the oil to the pot and stir in the onions and garlic with the salt. Sauté until soft.

3. Mix in the rice and cook for 2 minutes before adding the vegetables, layer style, on top, i.e. carrot, turnip, daikon radish, cabbage.

4. Gently pour in the water and add ⅓ teaspoon salt.

5. Tightly cover the pot and bake in a pre-heated oven at 350°F/180°C/gas mark 4 for 1½ hours or until the water is absorbed. If rice is still undercooked, add ½ pint (280ml) boiling vegetable stock, re-cover and bake for a further ½ hour, or until soft.

6. Serve hot with whole cooked beans or lentils and nori condiment (p. 87).

OVEN RICE

This is a good method of cooking rice for those at work all day, and for saving on fuel costs.

6 oz (170g) short grain brown rice
12 fl oz (340ml) water
Pinch of sea salt

1. Preheat the oven to 375°F/190°C/gas mark 5.

2. Wash and drain the rice and add to a pot with the measured water and the sea salt.

3. Bring to the boil with a lid on the pot, and simmer for 15 minutes.

4. Turn the rice and water into a preheated 1½ pint (840ml) ovenproof casserole, cover and place in the preheated oven.

5. Turn off the oven heat and leave the dish in the oven for 3-4 hours, or overnight. The rice will steam cook and will be ready to eat, perfectly cooked.

TRAVELLER'S RICE

**6 oz (170g) brown rice
12 fl oz (340ml) water
1-1½ umeboshi plums (p. 84)**

1. Cook the rice with the water and the umeboshi plums in a heavy pot with a tightly fitting lid until all the water is absorbed. This rice keeps longer than normal without refrigeration (3-5 days) in cold weather, and is particularly suitable for anyone with a poor digestion or a poor appetite.

2. It is especially nourishing and tasty when served with toasted sunflower seeds and finely cut spring onions.

BROWN RICE WITH CHESTNUTS (CHRISTMAS RICE)

**6 oz (170g) short-grain brown rice
12 fl oz (340ml) water
Pinch of sea salt
8-10 dried chestnuts, pre-soaked overnight**

1. Wash the rice, add the water and salt, bring to the boil and then simmer for 40 minutes until cooked.

2. In a separate pot, bring the chestnuts in their soaking water to the boil, and simmer for 30 minutes until tender. If necessary, remove the dark skins prior to cooking.

3. Drain and chop the cooked chestnuts, either finely or in quarters, and mix with the cooked rice in a mixing bowl.

4. Serve with lightly cooked Brussels sprouts and a flavoursome mixture of sautéed vegetables, such as onions, carrots and mushrooms.

Variation:
This recipe can also be used to make Rice and Chestnut Croquettes.

1. Chop the chestnuts finely before mixing with the rice.

2. Dampen the hands to form the rice-chestnut mixture into croquettes and either bake, shallow-fry or serve cold with salad.

STIR-FRY RICE

**2 teaspoons oil
2 oz (55g) finely sliced onion
Pinch of sea salt
2 oz (55g) carrot matchsticks
1 lb 2 oz (500g) cooked brown rice (p. 37)
2 oz (55g) radish, finely sliced
2 oz (55g) diced green leaves (from radish, cauliflower, turnip tops, daikon, etc.) or parsley**

1. Heat a large shallow pan or wok and add 2 teaspoons oil (or lightly brush with oil using a pastry brush).

2. Stir in the onion with a pinch of sea salt and cook until soft.

3. Add the carrots, then the rice, and finally the radish and greens. Cook for 2-3 minutes, stirring continuously.

4. Turn into a preheated serving dish and serve with Pressed Salad (p. 74), Chinese leaves, cucumber, Sauerkraut (p. 80), etc. Toasted nuts or seeds in shoyu sauce combine well with this dish.

VEGETABLE PAELLA

¾ lb (340g) brown rice
1⅕ pints (680ml) water
3 onions, finely sliced
½ tablespoon oil
Pinch of sea salt
1 clove garlic, minced (optional)
1 stalk celery, finely sliced
¼ diced red pepper (optional)
1 ear sweetcorn
3 oz (85g) fresh peas
Pinch of ground bay leaf
Pinch of saffron (optional)
Sprig of parsley, freshly chopped
3 spring onions, finely sliced

1. Boil the rice in lightly salted water (with the saffron, if used) for 40 minutes, until all the water is absorbed.

2. Sauté the onion in the oil with a pinch of sea salt, then add the garlic, celery, red pepper, sweetcorn and peas.

3. Stir the ground bay leaf into the vegetables.

4. Arrange the rice in a ring with a hollow centre, and fill with the vegetables.

5. Garnish with the parsley and spring onions.

FRUIT AND VEGETABLE CURRY

4 stalks celery, chopped
1 onion, chopped
½ teaspoon sea salt
1 tablespoon oil
1 tablespoon curry powder (p. 83)
1 tablespoon barley flour
½ pint (280ml) vegetable stock or water
1 teaspoon fresh grated ginger root
1 lemon, rind and juice
4 oz (110g) chopped, dried apricots
2 bananas, thickly sliced (optional)
1 lb (455g) cooking apples, peeled and cored
4 oz (110g) raisins
¼ pint (140ml) natural yogurt or sour cream

1. Sauté the celery and onion with the salt in the oil until golden, but do not brown.

2. Stir in the curry powder and flour, and add the stock and the ginger.

3. Add the juice and rind of the lemon, the apricots, bananas, apples and raisins. Cook gently.

4. Just before serving, add the sour cream or yogurt.

5. Serve with boiled brown rice.

MILLET, CARROT AND ONION SAVOURY

6 oz (170g) millet
1 onion, finely chopped
1-2 teaspoons oil (optional)
4 oz (110g) diced carrot, sweetcorn,
courgette or cauliflower, etc.
¼ teaspoon sea salt or yeast extract
1⅕ pints (680ml) water

1. Wash and drain the millet.

2. Sauté or simmer the onion for 5 minutes.

3. Add the carrot, millet, salt and water.
Bring to the boil and simmer, covered, for
30-35 minutes, until the grain is light and
fluffy and all the water is absorbed.

4. Turn into a rectangular 3 inch (7.5cm)
deep baking tin and allow to cool.

5. Slice and serve with a seasonal salad, or
serve hot with lightly cooked leafy green
vegetables and Bean Sauce (p. 92).

Variation: Optional extras include toasted
sunflower seeds, or finely grated white
Cheddar cheese, added to the cooked millet
before removing from the pot.
The mixture can also be formed into millet
balls and rolled in toasted sesame seeds.
The balls can be served hot, by re-heating
the oven or shallow frying. Served cold, they
are excellent for picnics and packed
lunches.

MILLET BAKE

6 oz (170g) millet
18 fl oz (500ml) water
1 teaspoon sea salt
1 onion sliced
4 oz (110g) mushrooms, sliced
2 teaspoons oil
1 tablespoon roasted barley flour
¾ pint (420ml) vegetable stock, seasoned
with tamari/shoyu soya sauce

1. Cook the millet in the water for 30
minutes with the salt.

2. When cooked, transfer to an ovenproof
dish.

3. To make the sauce, lightly sauté the onion
and the mushrooms in the oil.

4. Stir in the flour and gradually add the
vegetable stock. Bring to the boil, stirring to
thicken.

5. Pierce the millet with a skewer all over the
surface and cover with the sauce. Place in an
oven preheated to 350°F/180°C/gas mark
4, and bake for 30 minutes.

6. Serve with plenty of lightly steamed green
vegetables, and garnish with toasted
sunflower seeds.

ONE POT MILLET AND VEGETABLES

This recipe is good with chicken in place of
stuffing.

6 oz (170g) millet (dry-roasted if wished)
½ lb (225g) finely cut leeks or onions
4 oz (110g) finely cut broccoli or white
cabbage
2 teaspoons yeast extract
18 fl oz (500ml) vegetable stock
2 oz (55g) sunflower seeds
1 bay leaf

1. Put the millet into a pot with a tightly fitting lid and cover with the vegetables.

2. Dissolve the yeast extract in the stock and add with the sunflower seeds and bay leaf.

3. Bring to the boil and simmer for 30 minutes, until the millet is cooked and the stock is absorbed.

4. Serve with boiled or steamed Brussels sprouts.

Variation: For extra flavour, top this dish with sautéed onions and mushrooms, puréed chick peas or Bean Sauce (p. 92), or Ginger Sauce (p. 89).

MILLET SOUFFLÉ

1 medium onion, finely sliced
½ teaspoon sea salt
1 dessertspoon oil
1 medium carrot, diced
4 oz (110g) millet
12 fl oz (340ml) water and 1 teaspoon yeast extract
2 oz (55g) finely grated white Cheddar cheese (optional)
1 egg yolk (optional)
Pinch of dried thyme
2 egg whites (optional)
Breadcrumbs, as necessary

1. Sauté the onion with the salt in the oil until golden, then add the diced carrot and the washed and drained millet.

2. Stir to mix, then add the water and yeast extract.

3. Cover, bring to the boil and simmer for 30-35 minutes until all the water is absorbed and the grain is cooked.

4. Allow to cool, then fork and mix with the cheese, egg yolk and thyme.

5. Beat the egg whites until peaked and fold into the mixture.

6. Turn into a shallow ovenproof soufflé or similar dish. (The mixture should be approximately 3 inches [7.5cm] deep.)

7. Sprinkle with mixed grain breadcrumbs and finely grated white cheese, then bake in a preheated oven at 375°F/190°C/gas mark 5 for 20-30 minutes.

Note: This recipe can be made without the cheese and eggs.

BUCKWHEAT AND MISO STEW

1 lb (455g) vegetables (carrot, turnip, parsnip, onion, leek, etc.), finely sliced
1 tablespoon oil (optional)
1½ pints (840ml) water or vegetable stock
6 oz (170g) roasted buckwheat
4 teaspoons miso

1. Sauté or simmer the vegetables until just cooked.

2. Add the water or stock, bring to the boil, cover and simmer gently for 10 minutes.

3. Add the buckwheat to the stew.

4. Dissolve the miso in a little stew stock, add to the stew, and simmer for a further 20 minutes at least. The stew should be thick and mushy.

BUCKWHEAT AND VEGETABLE PIE

1 large onion, chopped
1 green or red pepper, chopped (optional)
1 tablespoon oil
Pinch of sea salt
½lb (225g) sliced mushrooms (optional)
10oz (280g) diced vegetables (carrot, turnip, cauliflower)
½lb (225g) roasted buckwheat
1 clove crushed garlic
1 teaspoon oregano
1 pint (570ml) boiling water
1-2 teaspoons miso to taste
1½oz (45g) grated white cheese (optional)
1oz (28g) rye breadcrumbs

1. Preheat the oven to 375°F/190°C/gas mark 5.

2. Sauté the onion and pepper in the oil with the salt, add the mushrooms, the diced vegetables and the roasted buckwheat and cook gently for about 5 minutes.

3. Stir in the garlic and the oregano, add the water, bring to the boil and simmer gently for 15-20 minutes, until the buckwheat is cooked.

4. Taste, and if required, add the miso dissolved in a little hot water, stirring well.

5. Transfer to a lightly greased pie dish, and sprinkle with the grated cheese and breadcrumbs.

6. Bake for 20-30 minutes at 375°F/190°C/gas mark 5, until topping is golden.

BUCKWHEAT SAVOURY

1 onion, sliced
2 pints (1.1 litres) vegetable or kombu seaweed stock
2 carrots, cubed
6oz (170g) roasted buckwheat
Pinch of sea salt

1. Simmer the onion in 1 cup of stock until just tender.

2. Add the carrots and the buckwheat, the remainder of the stock and the salt.

3. Cover and simmer for 15-20 minutes until the water is absorbed and the grain is soft.

4. Serve with Tamari Gravy (p. 89) or Arrowroot Sauce (p. 89).

ADUKI BEAN AND MUSHROOM PIE

6oz (170g) cooked aduki beans (p. 00)
6oz (170g) mushrooms
3 stalks celery, chopped
1 clove garlic, finely chopped
1 tablespoon cold-pressed oil
1 tablespoon tamari/shoyu soya sauce
1 tablespoon chopped parsley
1 teaspoon ginger juice
1 tablespoon tahini
4oz (110g) shortcrust pastry case (p. 107)

1. Mash the beans.

2. Sauté the mushrooms, celery and garlic in a little oil, then mix with the beans and other ingredients.

3. Put the bean and mushroom filling into the pastry case, and bake for 30 minutes at 400°F/200°C/gas mark 6.

LENTIL PIE

4 oz (110g) shortcrust pastry (see recipe
p.107)
1 large onion, sliced
1 tablespoon oil
Sea salt to taste
3 oz (85g) mushrooms
5 oz (140g) cooked lentils (p. 37)
1 tablespoon parsley, freshly chopped
2 oz (55g) white Cheddar cheese
(optional)
1 egg (optional)
1 tomato (optional)

1. Preheat the oven to 425°F/220°C/gas
mark 7.

2. Use the pastry to line an 8 inch (20cm)
flan or pie dish. Prick the base and bake
blind for 15 minutes.

3. Remove from the oven and allow to cool.
Turn the oven down to 350°F/180°C/
gas mark 4.

4. Sauté the onion in the oil with the salt
until tender, add the mushrooms and cook
for a further 3-5 minutes.

5. Remove from the heat. Stir in the lentils
and the parsley, mix in the cheese and the
beaten egg and adjust the seasoning as
required.

6. Put the mixture into the pastry case, top
with the finely sliced tomato and bake for
30-40 minutes.

BEAN AND TOMATO PIE

1 large onion, sliced
2 tablespoons oil
½ lb (225g) tomatoes, peeled and sliced
½ teaspoon basil
½ teaspoon sage
½ teaspoon marjoram
½ lb (225g) cooked haricot beans (p. 37)
6 oz (170g) shortcrust pastry (p. 107)
3 oz (85g) grated cheese (optional)

1. Sauté the onion in the oil, then add the
tomatoes and cook for a few more minutes.

2. Add the herbs and the cooked beans and
leave for 10 minutes to blend the flavours.
Allow to cool.

3. Use two-thirds of the pastry to line a fairly
deep well-greased baking dish.

4. Put in the filling, and cover with the
remaining pastry cut into 1 inch (2.5cm)
strips and used to make a lattice design, or
simply top with grated cheese.

5. Bake in a hot oven, 400°F/200°C/gas
mark 6, for 30-40 minutes.

LEFTOVER, OR SECOND-DAY BEANS

Almost as good as second-day soup.

1 tablespoon oil
1 clove garlic, minced, or ½ cup finely
sliced spring onions
½ onion, diced
Pinch of sea salt
1 lb (455g) cooked beans, drained of the
bean stock
6 oz (170g) cooked brown rice, barley or
oats (optional)
3½ fl oz (100ml) natural yogurt (optional)
Pinch of thyme or mixed herbs

1. Heat a heavy pot and brush with oil.

2. Add the garlic, onion and salt and sauté
for 2-3 minutes.

3. Add the beans and the grains, mash well,
and sauté for 3-4 minutes until slightly dry
and crisp.

4. Remove from the heat and stir in the
yogurt and herbs.

5. Serve with lightly steamed greens or salad.

BEANBURGERS

1 onion, chopped
1 green pepper, chopped, or 6 oz (170g)
celery, sliced
1 clove garlic, crushed (optional)
1-2 teaspoons oil
½ lb (225g) black-eyed beans, cooked
(p. 37)
2 oz (55g) rye breadcrumbs
1 tablespoon sesame tahini (optional)
Sea salt to taste
Breadcrumbs or sesame seeds for coating

1. Sauté the vegetables in the oil.

2. Drain the beans, reserving the stock, mash them and mix all the ingredients together using the breadcrumbs to thicken the mixture.

3. Season to taste.

4. Form into burgers and coat with breadcrumbs or sesame seeds. Shallow fry on both sides, or cook as Grillburgers (p. 71)

STEAMED SAVOURY DUMPLING

Served with blanched cauliflower, broccoli or carrot flowers and tamari/shoyu/brown rice vinegar dressing, this dish is a true delicacy.

½ lb (225g) cooked brown lentils (p. 37)
½ lb (225g) barley flakes
1 tablespoon gomasio sesame salt or ½
tablespoon gomasio and ½ tablespoon
tahini sesame cream
1 teaspoon yeast extract

1. Drain the lentils, keeping the cooking water.

2. Mash the lentils, then mix in the flakes and the gomasio, and add sufficient of the lentil cooking water to give a soft mixture.

3. Put into a steaming bowl, cover, and steam for 45 minutes to 1 hour.

4. Remove the bowl from the steaming pot and allow to cool slightly before running a knife around the inside of the bowl to release the heat.

5. Turn out on to a serving plate and serve hot with puréed vegetables, Arrowroot/ Kuzu Sauce (p. 89) or a bowl of soup.

6. Alternately, allow to cool, slice and serve with a seasonal salad. This is ideal for packed lunches.

Variation: The flavour of the dumpling can be varied by using different pulses and grains, for example, chick peas and oats, aduki beans and brown rice, etc. The addition of finely chopped vegetables also gives flavour and moistness. Herbs, e.g. chopped parlsey, either dried or fresh, or finely chopped seaweeds such as dulse, wakame or nori flakes, can also be added, if desired.

VEGETABLE AND LENTIL STEW

2 onions, sliced
1½ tablespoons oil (optional)
Sea salt or tamari/shoyu soya sauce to
taste
1 lb (455g) mixed root vegetables –
swede, parsnip, turnip, peeled and diced
1½ sticks celery, sliced
½ lb (225g) green or brown lentils
1-2 bay leaves
6 inch (15cm) strip of kombu seaweed
1½ pints (840ml) vegetable stock
1 tablespoon arrowroot or kuzu
½ tablespoon parsley

1. Sauté or simmer the onions with a pinch of sea salt until tender.

2. Add the vegetables and cook gently for a further 5 minutes.

3. Stir in the lentils, add the bay leaves, kombu and stock, cover and simmer for about 20 minutes until the vegetables and lentils are soft.

4. Remove the kombu, add the shoyu or sea salt to taste, and simmer for a further 5-10 minutes.

5. Drain, and thicken the gravy with the arrowroot or kuzu and stir back into the dish.

6. Sprinkle with parsley and serve with brown rice or jacket potatoes or, with a savoury crumble topping (p. 00), crisped in the oven or toasted under the grill.

Note: To give a creamy type of sauce, 7 fl oz (200ml) natural yogurt can be added at the end of cooking.

BROWN LENTIL RISOTTO

**1 large onion
1 teaspoon oil
1 teaspoon sea salt
1½ lb (670g) cooked brown rice (p. 37)
¾ lb (340g) cooked brown lentils (p. 37)
1 tablespoon parsley, finely chopped**

1. Lightly sauté or simmer the onion with a pinch of salt.

2. Add the rice and the lentils and heat through.

3. Garnish with the parsley and serve with lightly cooked fresh greens and carrot slices.

WINTER BEAN HOT-POT

**1 large onion
½ pint (280ml) bean stock
1 teaspoon sea salt
½ lb (225g) cooked beans (p. 37)
¾ lb (340g) cauliflower sprigs
4 oz (110g) sliced carrot
2 teaspoons tahini**

1. Slice the onion and simmer in the bean stock with the salt, until tender.

2. Add the beans, cauliflower sprigs, sliced carrot and tahini, and cook for 30 minutes over a low heat.

3. Turn into a heated casserole and serve.

KOMBU, ADUKI BEAN AND PUMPKIN DISH

**3 strips kombu seaweed, pre-soaked for 10 minutes, and cut into 1 inch (2.5cm) square pieces
6 oz (170g) aduki beans, pre-soaked
1 pint (570ml) water
2 lb (900g) pumpkin, peeled and chopped into 2 inch (5cm) chunks
Tamari/shoyu soya sauce to taste**

1. Place the kombu in the bottom of a small heavy pot, top with the aduki beans and cover with the water.

2. Cover the pot with the lid, bring to the boil, boil for 10 minutes, then simmer for 20 minutes.

3. Place the pumpkin chunks on top of the kombu and aduki beans.

4. Cover and continue to cook for another 20 minutes, until both the beans and the pumpkin are soft. If the water runs low, add a little more liquid to ensure that the dish does not become dry.

5. In the last 2-3 minutes of cooking add a little tamari or shoyu sauce to flavour lightly.

6. Serve with plain cooked grain (p. 37) and lightly steamed greens.

Beans with Onions and Celery

1 head of celery
1 onion
½-1 tablespoon oil
Pinch of sea salt
½-1 teaspoon dried herbs
½ lb (225g) cooked beans (p. 37)
Tamari/shoyu soya sauce to taste
1 tablespoon arrowroot/kuzu starch
¾ lb (340g) cooked brown rice, millet or
buckwheat (p. 37)
1½ tablespoons chopped parsley

1. Wash and cut the celery into 1 inch (2.5cm) diagonal slices.

2. Slice the onion and sauté in the oil with a pinch of salt, for about 5 minutes.

3. Add the celery and the dried herbs and mix well.

4. Cover and cook slowly over a medium heat.

5. Drain the stock off the beans. Mix the beans with the vegetables and heat through.

6. Reheat and season the bean stock made up to ½ pint (280ml) and thicken with the arrowroot or kuzu, dissolved in a little cold water.

7. Serve the bean dish on brown rice, millet or buckwheat, pour on the sauce and garnish with the parsley.

Red Kidney Bean Casserole

½ lb (225g) dried kidney beans
1¼ pints (700ml) water
3 carrots, cubed
3 onions, thickly sliced
1 bay leaf
¼ teaspoon sea salt

1. Soak the beans overnight. Rinse and add the measured water.

2. Bring to the boil and boil for 10 minutes, then simmer for 40 minutes.

3. Add the carrots, onions, bay leaf and salt, and simmer for a further 20 minutes.

4. Serve with boiled brown rice and lightly cooked green vegetables.

Beanfeast

1 large onion
1 large carrot
1 clove garlic (optional)
1 tablespoon oil
2 allspice berries, crushed (optional)
½ lb (225g) cooked red kidney beans
(p. 37)
Large pinch of dried ginger or 2 inch
(5cm) piece of fresh ginger, sliced
4 oz (110g) cooked brown rice or barley
(p. 37)
Juice of ½ lemon
2 tablespoons apple juice
1-2 large tomatoes (optional)
1-2 courgettes
Few sprigs of cauliflower
1 teaspoon yeast extract dissolved in
½ pint (280ml) water

1. Slice the onion and chop the carrot into chunks, crush the garlic, and sauté all three in a little cold-pressed oil for a few minutes.

2. Add the spice and cook for about one minute longer.

3. Add the cooked beans and all the other ingredients.

4. Simmer for 30 minutes.

BEAN OR LENTIL SUPREME

1 onion, sliced
1-2 teaspoons oil
Sea salt to taste
½ lb (225g) mushrooms, quartered
½ teaspoon dried herbs
½ lb (225g) cooked beans or lentils (p. 37)
3½ oz (100g) natural yogurt or cottage
cheese (optional)
Tamari/shoyu soya sauce to taste
¾ lb (340g) cooked brown rice or millet
(p. 37)
½ tablespoon freshly chopped parsley
1 tablespoon toasted sunflower seeds

1. Sauté the onions gently in the oil with a pinch of sea salt, then add the mushrooms and the dried herbs.

2. When soft, stir in the cooked beans or lentils and the yogurt or cottage cheese.

3. Heat through gently, adjust the seasoning and serve on a bed of cooked rice or millet.

4. Garnish with the parsley and sunflower seeds, and serve with lightly cooked carrots.

PULSE AND POTATO HOT-POT

1 lb (455g) potatoes
3 onions, sliced
½ lb (225g) cooked beans (aduki etc.),
split peas or lentils (p. 37)
1-2 teaspoons miso or yeast extract
¾ pint (420ml) warm water or stock

1. Par-boil the potatoes, then slice and place with the onions in a well-greased pie dish layered with beans or lentils. The top layer should be potatoes.

2. Dissolve the miso in the warm water and pour over the beans and potatoes.

3. Cover and bake in a moderate oven, 350°F/180°C/gas mark 4, until tender, about an hour. Brown with the lid off.

4. Garnish, if liked, with finely grated white cheese or toasted nuts and seeds, and serve with lightly steamed green vegetables.

BEAN AND VEGETABLE HOT-POT

1 large onion
½ tablespoon sunflower oil
Sea salt to taste
6 inch (15cm) piece of kombu seaweed
1 lb (455g) cooked beans of choice
(p. 37)
1 bay leaf
2 medium carrots, cubed
2 potatoes, quartered, skins left on
4 stalks celery plus leaves
Pinch of thyme or marjoram
4-6 Brussels sprouts
¾ pint (420ml) vegetable stock, well
flavoured with miso or yeast extract

1. Finely slice the onion and sauté in the oil with a pinch of sea salt.

2. Soak the kombu for 5 minutes and then cut into 1 inch (2.5cm) pieces.

3. Place on top of the onions and add the beans.

4. Now add the vegetables in the following order – bay leaf, carrots, potatoes, celery, dried herbs, Brussels sprouts.

5. Pour in the vegetable stock and cook for 45 minutes in the oven at 400°F/200°C/gas mark 6.

6. Drain off the stock, thicken with arrowroot or kuzu, and serve poured over the hot-pot.

Home-baked Beans and Rice

1 lb (455g) cooked beans (choose from
black-eyed beans, soya beans, haricot
beans etc.) – p. 37
1½ lb (670g) cooked brown rice (p. 37)
10 oz (280g) diced onions, leeks or
spring onions
2½ tablespoons tomato purée (optional)
or 6 oz (170g) grated carrot
12 fl oz (340ml) bean stock
1 teaspoon fresh mustard (optional)
3 teaspoons miso or yeast extract

1. Combine the beans, rice, onions, tomato
purée and bean stock in a pot and heat
through.

2. Add the mustard and miso to taste.

3. Cook for a further 5-10 minutes to blend
the flavours.

4. Serve hot with mashed turnip, lightly
boiled greens and more boiled rice, or cold
with a seasonal salad.

Vegetarian Shepherd's Pie

½ lb (225g) whole green or brown lentils
6 oz (170g) pot (whole) barley
6 inch (15cm) strip of kombu seaweed
1 pint (570ml) water
1 onion
1 clove garlic, crushed (optional)
2 medium carrots, chopped
6 oz (170g) walnuts
Tamari/shoyu soya sauce to taste
1 lb (455g) potatoes (steamed and mashed)
2 oz (55g) cheese, grated (optional)

1. Simmer the lentils and pot barley with the
kombu in the water, for 30 minutes.

2. Add the onion, garlic, carrots and walnuts
and cook for a further 20 minutes until
everything is tender.

3. Season with tamari/shoyu as required.

4. Top with mashed potato and grated
cheese and place in oven. Bake at
350°F/180°C/gas mark 4 for 30 minutes or
until browned on top.

Note: Parsley and other herbs can be used to
vary the flavour. Also use celery, leeks,
turnips etc., as available.

Vegetable and Lentil Crumble

2 onions, sliced
1 tablespoon oil
Sea salt to taste
½ lb (225g) green or brown lentils
¾ pint (420ml) water or vegetable stock
1-2 bay leaves
6 inch (15cm) strip of kombu seaweed
Juice of ½ fresh lemon (optional)
¾ lb (340g) carrot, celery or fennel
4 oz (110g) rye breadcrumbs
2 oz (55g) white cheese, finely grated
(optional), *or* sunflower seeds or flaked
almonds

1. Sauté or simmer the onion for 5 minutes
with a little salt.

2. Add the lentils, stock or water, bay leaves
and kombu, bring to the boil and simmer
gently for 20-30 minutes.

3. Remove the kombu and the bay leaves.
Drain off excess stock and liquidize or sieve
the lentils.

4. Add the lemon juice and adjust the
seasoning as required.

5. Preheat the oven to 375°F/190°C/gas mark 5.

6. Wash the vegetables and slice into chunks and cook in a little unsalted water until just tender. Drain well and reserve the stock.

7. Lightly grease a shallow ovenproof casserole. Put the vegetables in the bottom of the dish, cover with the lentil mixture and top with the breadcrumbs and cheese (or seeds or almonds).

8. Bake for 30-40 minutes until the top is crunchy and golden and the mixture is hot and bubbling.

BUTTER BEAN CRUMBLE

3 stalks celery, chopped
1 onion, sliced
2 large carrots, diced
1 tablespoon oil
1 tablespoon flour, rye, barley or organically-grown whole wheat
½ pint (280ml) vegetable stock
Sea salt to taste
3 oz (85g) grated cheese (optional)
6 oz (170g) cooked butter beans (p. 37)
2 oz (55g) rolled oats

1. Sauté the vegetables in the oil for a few minutes, then stir in the flour.

2. Gradually add the stock, stirring continually, to make a creamy sauce.

3. Adjust the seasoning and add 2 oz (55g) of the cheese, if used.

4. Place the cooked beans in an ovenproof dish and cover with the sauce.

5. Top with rolled oats and grated cheese or flaked nuts or seeds.

6. Bake for 25 minutes at 400°F/200°C/gas mark 6.

BEAN LOAF

1 onion, sliced
1 clove garlic, crushed or ½ bunch spring onions, finely sliced
1-2 teaspoons oil
4 oz (110g) mushrooms, chopped or ½ pint (280ml) thick, well flavoured mushroom sauce, if not using tomato or egg (see p. 91)
½ lb (225g) cooked beans (aduki, pinto, black-eyed beans, etc. – p. 37
4 oz (110g) barley flakes, rye breadcrumbs or cooked rice (p. 37)
1 teaspoon thyme
2 teaspoons tamari/shoyu soya sauce
4 oz (110g) tomatoes, chopped (optional)
1 egg (optional)
Pinch of sea salt

1. Sauté the onion and the garlic or spring onions in a little oil, and add the mushrooms.

2. Mash half the beans and mix all the ingredients together.

3. Put into a lightly greased loaf tin and bake for 35 minutes at 375°F/190°C/gas mark 5.

MEATLESS SAVOURY LOAF

6 oz (170g) cooked green or brown lentils
(p. 37)
4 oz (110g) ground hazelnuts, almonds
or sunflower seeds
4 oz (110g) oat or barley flakes or rye
breadcrumbs
½ teaspoon mixed dried herbs
½ teaspoon thyme
½ teaspoon oregano
2 onions, sliced
1 clove garlic, crushed (optional)
2 carrots, diced
2 sticks of celery, chopped
½ chopped red or green pepper (optional)
2 teaspoons oil
1 beaten egg (optional) or ¼ pint
(140ml) vegetable/bean stock
Sea salt or miso to taste

1. Combine the lentils with the nuts,
oatflakes and herbs.

2. Sauté the onion, garlic and other
vegetables in the oil until golden, or simmer
in a little stock.

3. Stir the vegetables into the lentil mixture,
add the beaten egg, if used, or a little stock
to bind, and season to taste with sea salt or
miso.

4. Turn into a lightly greased meat-loaf tin,
and bake for 40 minutes at 375°F/190°C/
gas mark 5.

5. Serve hot with brown rice and sauerkraut
or cold with a tossed green salad.

PRAWN OR SHRIMP RISOTTO

6 oz (170g) finely sliced onion
1 tablespoon sesame or sunflower oil
Pinch of sea salt
6 oz (170g) shrimps or prawns, boiled
1½ lb (670g) cooked brown rice (p. 37)
1-2 teaspoons brown rice vinegar or
apple cider vinegar
Tamari/shoyu soya sauce to taste
Fresh parsley sprigs or watercress

1. Sauté the onion in the oil, with a pinch of
sea salt, until soft.

2. Add the shrimps or prawns, whole or
halved, according to size and preference.

3. Stir-fry to heat through, then add the rice.
Mix and heat thoroughly.

4. Add the brown rice vinegar to give a tangy
flavour if liked, and season, if required.

5. Serve in a preheated ovenproof dish
garnished with fresh parsley or sprigs of
watercress.

GRILLED HERRING

2 lb (900g) fresh herring, filleted
Pinch of sea salt
2 fresh oranges or Cox's orange pippin
apples
1 tablespoon fresh parsley, finely chopped

1. Wash and dry the herring and place, skin
side down, on the grill pan. Season with the
salt.

2. Grill gently for 15 minutes until tender,
turning to cook evenly.

3. Slice the oranges or apples and place over
the herring. Grill for a further 2-3 minutes.

4. Serve with boiled potatoes and garnished
with parsley.

OATMEAL HERRINGS

3-4 cardamom pods
2 lb (900g) fresh herrings, filleted
Fine oatmeal for coating
Pinch each of dried or fresh parsley,
oregano and tarragon
Pinch of sea salt
1 tablespoon oil (optional)

1. Crush the cardamom pods and rub over the herrings.

2. Mix the oatmeal, herbs and salt and roll the herring in the mixture to coat.

3. Bake, grill or shallow-fry.

FRESH RIVER TROUT

1 trout per person, filleted
1 fresh eating apple
2 tablespoons butter or oil
2 teaspoons fresh or dried herbs of
choice
2 tablespoons flaked almonds, lightly
toasted

1. Carefully wash and dry the trout, removing the head and tail if wished.

2. Finely slice the apple, insert into the fish and place on a baking tray.

3. Cream the butter and herbs and dot over the outside of the fish. Cook gently under the grill or in a medium oven for 10-15 minutes, until the flesh is pink and tender.

4. Sprinkle with the almonds and serve with lightly cooked vegetables or salad.

ONE POT POACHED FISH AND VEGETABLES

1 large onion or 1 medium leek, sliced
6 oz (170g) carrot, sliced
1 stalk of celery or a small bulb of fennel,
cut diagonally
½ teaspoon fennel seed (if not using a
fennel bulb)
6 oz (170g) broccoli sprigs, cauliflower
sprigs or sweetcorn kernels
6 fl oz (170ml) vegetable stock or water
seasoned to taste with yeast extract
1 lb (455g) fresh fish fillets (haddock,
sole, whiting)
1 tablespoon arrowroot/kuzu
1 tablespoon fresh parsley or chives

1. Simmer the vegetables for 10 minutes in the stock.

2. Rinse and dry the fish, roll lengthwise and place on top of the bed of simmering vegetables.

3. Re-cover the pot and gently poach the fish for a further 10 minutes, until just tender.

4. Remove the fish to a serving dish, drain the vegetables and arrange them around the fish.

5. Taste the stock and adjust the seasoning if required. Lightly thicken with arrowroot or kuzu and pour over the fish. Garnish with freshly chopped parsley or chives.

Note: In place of yeast extract and fennel, this dish can be given an oriental flavour by using tamari/shoyu soya sauce and freshly grated ginger root. Serve the fish and vegetables on a bed of brown rice and glaze with the stock, thickened as above.

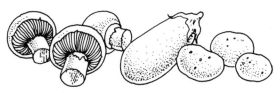

BAKED SALMON OR TROUT

½ lb (225g) onions, sliced
1 tablespoon oil (optional)
Pinch of sea salt
½ lb (225g) cooked brown rice (p. 37)
1 fresh salmon or trout
2-3 teaspoons butter or oil mixed with
fresh chopped herbs or fennel seeds
4 oz (110g) button mushrooms

1. Sauté or simmer the onion with the salt, until tender.

2. Mix with the rice and spread over the bottom of a long ovenproof dish.

3. Wash and dry the cleaned fish, place on top of the rice and dot with the herb butter.

4. Wash the mushrooms and use to stuff the fish.

5. Cover and bake for 30-40 minutes at 350°F/180°C/gas mark 4.

6. Serve hot or cold with lightly steamed broccoli sprigs, Brussels sprouts, cauliflower, or Chinese leaves and a garnish of fresh lemon wedges or dill pickle (p. 80).

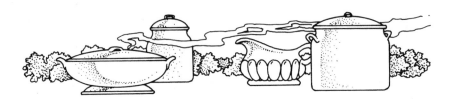

Snacks and Quick Meals

Between-meal snacks are, in theory at least, best discouraged for improved appetite at mealtimes. However, busy families involved in sports, school and eating away from home often find the need for nourishing, but easy-to-carry and easy-to-eat snack meals. Fast-food restaurants rarely provide low-fat, high-fibre, additive-free and wheat-free foods. Generally, the only alternative, when following a healthy wholefood programme, is to provide your own versions of fast-food, substituting nourishing and appropriate ingredients.

Some children (and adults) prefer eating a series of small meals rather than two or three meals in a day. Conventional snacks of biscuits, crisps, sweets, sugary drinks, salted nuts, chips and jam sandwiches satisfy the appetite but not all the body's nutrient needs.

The following suggestions are useful for those occasions when a quick mini-meal or picnic meal is called for. They require little preparation time and are often adapted from the previous day's main meal leftovers. Planning ahead, by making an extra portion of a favourite dish which can be refrigerated overnight, will supply you with an instant meal for those family members who materialize at odd hours accompanied by a ravenous appetite, proving that 'wholefood' can be fast food.

Suggestions For Quick Meals and Packed Lunches

Main ingredient
Meal in a Bowl Soup, p. 30, with a saucerful of seasonal salad.
Bean Spread, p. 32, on Mixed Grain Bread, p. 104, or Oatcakes, p. 115, with alfalfa sprouts, and other sandwiches, p. 68.
Slice of Sunflower and Almond Roast, p. 39, with Sauerkraut, p. 80.
Stuffed Cabbage Rolls, p. 45.
Rice Balls, p. 50.
Sushi Rice, p. 50.
Brown Rice Salad, p. 77.
Stir-fry Rice, p. 52.
Millet, Carrot and Onion Savoury, p. 54.
Onion Flan, p. 47.
Pumpkin Pie, p. 48.
Lentil Pie, p. 57.
Beanburgers, p. 58.
Buckwheat Burgers, p. 72.
Millet Croquettes, p. 70.
Millet Grillburgers, p. 71.
Pizza, p. 69.
Potato Patties, p. 70.

Afters, if desired
Nutty Biscuits, p. 118.
Almond and Apricot Crunchy Bar, p. 121.
Kirkintilloch Slices, p. 121.
Sunflower Seed Biscuits, p. 120.

Hot and cold drinks
Instant miso with spring onion or parlsey garnish.
Choice of soup, pp. 22 to 32.
Vegetable juice.
Unsweetened fruit juice (dilute to taste), hot or cold.
Grain 'coffees', p. 125.
Roasted dandelion root 'coffee', p. 123.
Bancha twig tea, p. 123.

SANDWICH FILLERS

1. Vegetable and bean spreads make excellent fillings that can be prepared in advance and used as required.

2. Beanspreads in toasted sandwiches make instant meals combined with a bowl of vegetable soup.

3. Walnuts and alfalfa sprouts placed between thin slices of rye bread spread with black-eyed bean spread make a tasty sandwich.

ITALIAN CHEESE BALLS

6 oz (170g) breadcrumbs
3 oz (85g) grated cheese
3 oz (85g) ground walnuts
1 teaspoon mixed herbs
1 small onion, grated
2 eggs
2-3 spring onions

1. Mix all the ingredients together.

2. Shape into balls and shallow fry or bake in the oven for 10-15 minutes at 350°F/180°C/gas mark 4, or place the mixture in a loaf tin and bake in the oven for 20 minutes at 350°F/180°C/gas mark 4.

COTTAGE CHEESE ROAST

½ lb (225g) cottage cheese
1 egg
2-3 spring onions or chives, chopped
½ lb (225g) raw grated carrot
1 tablespoon ground hazelnuts
Sea salt to taste
1 teaspoon mixed herbs

1. Mix all the ingredients together thoroughly.

2. Put into a greased loaf tin and bake at 350°F/180°C/gas mark 4, for 20-30 minutes, or until set.

3. Serve with a green salad or lightly steamed greens, or on a bed of boiled brown rice.

NUT CUTLETS

The uncooked mixture for these cutlets keeps well for 2-3 days if refrigerated, or it can be deep-frozen. All nuts in this recipe should be lightly toasted and the outer husks removed.

4 oz (110g) peanuts or sunflower seeds
4 oz (110g) hazelnuts
4 oz (110g) cashewnuts
½ lb (225g) onion, finely sliced and shallow-fried
2 eggs, hard boiled (optional) *or* use double quantity of carrot and potato
2 teaspoons tamari/shoyu soya sauce
2 oz (55g) carrot, boiled
2 oz (55g) potato, boiled
3 oz (85g) breadcrumbs or sesame seeds to coat

1. Finely mince or blend the nuts.

2. Blend in all remaining ingredients except the breadcrumbs. Taste and adjust the seasoning.

3. Mould into rounds or cutlets and toss in the coating.

4. Bake, grill or shallow-fry. Serve hot or cold.

CORN AND BEAN PATTIES

1 lb (455g) onions, shallow-fried in oil until soft
1 lb (455g) sweetcorn kernels, fresh or frozen
1 lb (455g) mashed potato, still warm
1 egg, beaten (optional)
1-4 tablespoons bean stock flavoured with yeast extract
Rye breadcrumbs, sesame seeds or finely ground sunflower seeds to coat

1. When the onions are soft, add the sweetcorn and stir to mix.

2. Stir in the freshly mashed potato, adding egg and/or bean stock if required, to bind. Form into rissoles or patties.

3. Roll in the breadcrumbs.

4. Bake in a medium oven, 350°F/180°C/ gas mark 4, or shallow-fry.

Variation: ½ lb (225g) cooked beans can be added for extra flavour and protein. Mash with the potato before mixing with the other ingredients.

BARLEY SCONE PIZZA

4 oz (110g) dairy-free margarine or butter
1 lb (455g) barley flour
Pinch of sea salt
2-3 teaspoons baking powder (p. 103)
Approximately ¼ pint (140ml) water to mix

Toppings:
Shallow-fried onion, cooked until tender
Shallow-fried onion with a selection of other vegetables such as mushrooms, carrot (grated), celery, sweetcorn, cauliflower, all cooked until tender
Fresh or tinned tomato
Cottage cheese
Finely grated white Cheddar or Edam cheese
Flaked nuts or seeds
Shrimps, prawns, sardines or cooked chicken

1. Rub the fat into the flour, salt and baking powder, then stir in the water to make a scone dough (not too soft).

2. Halve and roll out to 2 rounds ½ inch (1.2cm) thick. Place on a lightly greased baking tray and add your choice of topping.

3. Bake for 10-15 minutes at 425°F/220°C/ gas mark 7. When ready, the base will be a pale golden colour.

TRINA'S PRINCELY PIZZA

4 oz (110g) rye flour
½ lb (225g) barley flour
3 teaspoons baking powder (p. 103)
½ teaspoon sea salt
3 tablespoons oil
½ pint (280ml) milk

Topping:
2½ oz (70g) tomato purée
½ lb (225g) grated white cheese
¾ lb (340g) cooked mixed vegetables
(onion, carrot, celery) flavoured with
yeast extract, or a vegetable and pulse
mix

Plus a selection from:
2 oz (55g) prawns
2 oz (55g) pineapple cubes
3 oz (85g) mushrooms, sliced or quartered
as desired
2 oz (55g) red and/or green peppers,
sliced into rings
2 oz (55g) grated apple

1. Mix the flours, baking powder and salt.

2. Add the oil and milk and mix well,
kneading to form a smooth dough.

3. Divide into 2, and roll out on a floured
board to make 2 pizza bases, 10 inches
(25cm) in diameter and ½ inch (1.2cm)
thick.

4. Spread the base with a layer of tomato
purée.

5. Cover with a thick layer of grated cheese.

6. Top this with the vegetable, or vegetable-
pulse, mixture.

7. Add another layer of grated cheese and
top with prawns and pineapple, mushrooms
and red and green pepper rings or grated
apple as desired.

8. Bake for 15-20 minutes at 375°F/190°C/
gas mark 5.

POTATO AND VEGETABLE PATTIES

¾ lb (340g) mashed potato
6 oz (170g) left-over beans and vegetables
Miso or yeast extract to taste (optional)
Oatmeal for coating
Oil for shallow frying

1. Mash the potato, beans and vegetables
together and mix well.

2. Season if necessary, with a little miso or
yeast extract.

3. Form into patties and coat lightly with
oatmeal.

4. Shallow-fry until golden brown, about 3-
4 minutes each side.

MILLET CROQUETTES

1 lb 2 oz (500g) cooked millet (p. 37)
1 finely chopped onion, or spring onions
Pinch of sea salt
½ beaten egg (optional)
Sunflower or safflower oil for frying

1. In a large bowl combine the cooked
millet, the finely chopped raw onion or
spring onion and the salt. Mix well, pounding
with a wooden rolling pin or similar utensil.
A little egg may be added if liked.

2. Wet the hands and form the millet into
balls.

3. Shallow or deep fry in the oil. Fry small
batches at a time, using a lifting spoon to
separate the balls when first put into the oil.

4. Drain off excess oil and serve with Ginger
Shoyu Dip (p. 44).

MILLET GRILLBURGERS

These are usually very popular with children.

1-2 onions or a small bunch of spring
onions, finely sliced
¾ lb (340g) soft cooked millet (p. 37)
6 oz (170g) mashed potato
1 egg or 1 oz (28g) butter or dairy-free
margarine
1 teaspoon tomato purée (optional)
Sea salt or tamari/shoyu soya sauce to
taste
1 tablespoon sunflower oil (optional, for
shallow frying)

1. Use the onion lightly sautéed or raw, or
use finely sliced spring onions.

2. Combine the ingredients, lightly season
to taste (low salt for children), form into
burgers and toast under the grill or sautée.

3. Try the burgers tossed in toasted sesame
seeds. Serve hot or cold with salads or in
packed lunches.

4. Tasty accompaniments include sautéed
mushrooms, blanched, diced watercress,
Ginger Shoyu Dip (p. 44), Nori Condiment
(p. 87), Chunky Carrot Slices and Kombu
Crisps (p. 28).

SAVOURY FLAPJACKS

5 oz (140g) rolled oatflakes
1 oz (28g) sunflower seeds
1 oz (28g) sesame seeds
1 teaspoon fresh mustard paste (optional)
Pinch of cayenne pepper (optional)
4 oz (110g) white Cheddar or Cheshire
cheese, finely grated
1 free-range egg
2 tablespoons water or milk
3 oz (85g) butter, oil or dairy-free
margarine

1. Pre-heat the oven to 350°F/180°C/gas
mark 4.

2. Lightly grease an 8 inch (20cm) square,
shallow cake tin.

3. Combine the oats, seeds, spices and
cheese.

4. Beat the egg and water. Melt the butter
and stir into the dry ingredients with the egg
mixture.

5. Mix well, smooth into the prepared tin
and bake in the centre of the oven for 20-25
minutes until golden.

6. Mark into fingers and leave to cool in the
tin.

BUCKWHEAT BURGERS

6 oz (170g) roasted or unroasted
buckwheat
1 pint (570ml) water
Sea salt
1 onion and 1 leek, or 2 onions
1-2 teaspoons oil
2 stalks celery, chopped
1 carrot, finely grated
1 tablespoon freshly chopped parsley
Little rye flour

1. Add the buckwheat to the water with a pinch of salt.

2. Bring to the boil and simmer for 20 minutes, or until all the water is absorbed.

3. Sauté the onion in the oil with a pinch of salt, then add the leek, the celery and the carrot, and cook until just tender.

4. Allow to cool slightly, and mix the buckwheat with the vegetables, adding the freshly-cut parsley. Adjust the seasoning as required. A pinch of thyme may be added if liked.

5. Add a little rye flour to bind the ingredients, form into burgers and shallow-fry.

6. Garnish with finely chopped spring onion and thin slices of blanched red or green pepper. Serve with pressed salad or sauerkraut.

FISH FINGERS

½ lb (225g) cooked fish
¾ lb (340g) potato, boiled and mashed
1 ripe tomato, blanched and chopped or
1 teaspoon tomato purée
1-4 teaspoons tamari/shoyu soya sauce
or a pinch of sea salt
1 egg, beaten
4 oz (110g) breadcrumbs

1. Combine all the ingredients except for the egg and the breadcrumbs.

2. Gradually add the egg to bind the mixture. Do not make it too soft.

3. Divide the mixture evenly into 10-12 pieces and form into 'fingers'.

4. Coat in the breadcrumbs, and grill, bake or shallow-fry until crisp and golden.

Seasonal Salads

There are those who advocate eating a salad a day before a meal. Others maintain that raw food should not be consumed until after the meal, and then in small amounts only. What you do obviously depends on whether you have been eating a salad starter or raw-food meals for years and are in the peak of fitness. If so, then by all means continue, but remember that everything changes and that what is right for you here and now may alter with your age, lifestyle and location.

If, on the other hand, raw food has never featured in your life, then try introducing a little raw or blanched salad at the end, rather than at the beginning, of a meal.

The following recipes give some ideas for balanced and seasonal salads to use as starters or as an accompaniment to a main course dish.

BLANCHED SALAD

This can be used at any time of year, served at room temperature or lightly chilled.

Choose three of the following:
**3 oz (85g) cauliflower leaves, diced
1 small cauliflower, cut into sprigs
½ lb (225g) white cabbage
1 bunch watercress
1 lettuce
½ head celery
½ bunch spring onions
½ lb (225g) carrots, finely sliced or diced
6 oz (170g) radish, red or mooli
¾ lb (340g) Chinese leaves
3 oz (85g) broccoli, cut in sprigs**

1. Each vegetable should be blanched separately by plunging into unsalted boiling water for 1-4 minutes, in small batches.

2. Mix the vegetables in a bowl and serve with a separate dressing.

PRESSED SALAD

**10 inch (25cm) piece of cucumber
1 bunch spring onions
Small bunch radish
1 garden lettuce
1 teaspoon sea salt or 1-2 umeboshi plums**

1. Remove both ends from the cucumber and use the flat sides of these to rub the cut ends. This produces a white froth and removes any bitterness.

2. Slice the cucumber, spring onions, and radish, and chop the lettuce leaves very finely.

3. Mix all the ingredients including the salt or umeboshi plums together well, with the hand.

4. Cover and press for 2-6 hours to draw out the water.

5. Rinse to remove excess salt. Drain and serve.

Note: Pressing the salad ingredients in this way makes them easier to digest for those unused to raw vegetables. The same effect can be achieved by blanching the vegetables, or by adding a dressing made with ginger, spring onions, tamari/shoyu soya sauce or brown rice or umeboshi vinegars.

COLESLAW

**½ lb (225g) finely shredded white cabbage
1 oz (28g) very finely sliced onion or spring onion
6 inch (15cm) dulse, rinsed and finely sliced (optional)
4 oz (110g) diced fresh apple
1 oz (28g) soaked sultanas (optional)
Pinch of fennel seed (optional)**

Optional dressings:
Apple juice, apple cider vinegar, brown rice vinegar (p. 84), French Dressing (p. 88), 1 tablespoon natural yogurt

1. Mix the ingredients in a bowl. This will keep in a covered container for 1-2 days in the refrigerator but is best used fresh.

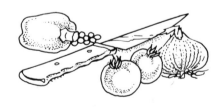

CRUNCHY CARROT AND BEETROOT SALAD

½ lb (225g) grated carrot
½ lb (225g) grated raw beetroot
4 oz (110g) celery, finely sliced
1 oz (28g) soaked sultanas
1 tablespoon apple juice
Dash of lemon juice

1. Mix all the ingredients together.

2. This salad is best used immediately but will keep in a covered container in the refrigerator for 1-2 days.

NORI AND SPROUT SALAD

2-3 sheets toasted nori
3 oz (85g) alfalfa sprouts
3 oz (85g) mung bean sprouts
4 oz (110g) sunflower seeds, toasted
6 oz (170g) grated carrot
2-3 teaspoons tamari/shoyu soya sauce
Juice of ½ fresh lemon or 1 tablespoon vinegar (p. 84)
1 tablespoon finely chopped fennel root (optional)
1 tablespoon chopped chives or spring onions (optional)

1. Toast the nori and cut into 1 inch (2.5cm) squares.

2. Combine the sprouts, toasted seeds and grated carrot and sprinkle with tamari/shoyu soya sauce, lemon juice and herbs.

3. Serve garnished with the nori squares.

WATERCRESS SALAD

1 bunch watercress
½ head garden lettuce
½ bunch radishes
3 oz (85g) beansprouts
½ lb (225g) cooked beans of choice
5 oz (140g) small cubes boiled tofu
(optional) or 2 oz (55g) toasted, flaked nuts or seeds

1. Wash the watercress, lettuce, radishes and beansprouts.

2. Chop the watercress, shred the lettuce and slice the radishes thinly.

3. Mix together with the beansprouts, and toss with the cooked beans and tofu.

4. Serve in individual bowls with Umeboshi Dressing (p. 88).

MIXED RAW SALAD

1 small cauliflower
1 red and 1 green pepper (optional)
2 stalks celery
4 oz (110g) mushrooms
½ cucumber
2 teaspoons parsley or finely chopped spring onions

1. Divide the cauliflower into small florets, dice the peppers, if used, slope-cut the celery and finely slice the mushrooms and cucumber.

2. Mix the ingredients together in a salad bowl.

3. Garnish with the parsley or spring onions, and serve with a French Dressing (p. 88) or an Umeboshi Plum Dressing (p. 88).

SAVOURY TOFU JELLY

This is a light summer dish which combines well with boiled brown rice, Wakame Salad (p. 42) and shredded Chinese leaves.

1 tablespoon Bonito dried fish flakes
(p. 83)
2 pints (1.1 litres) water or vegetable
stock
Tamari/shoyu sauce to taste
4 tablespoons agar-agar
Blanched carrot flowers
Blanched cucumber triangles
½ lb (225g) tofu

1. Add the fish flakes to the water or vegetable stock, bring to the boil and simmer for 3-5 minutes.

2. Remove the fish flakes, as these become bitter if left longer.

3. Flavour the stock with a little tamari, bring back to simmering and stir in the agar-agar, powder or flakes, the amount depending on the brand which you are using; generally, you need to use double the amount recommended on the packet.

4. Rinse a mould to dampen, and decorate with the carrot flowers and cucumber triangles. A 3 inch (7.5cm) deep rectangular dish is ideal.

5. Gently spoon sufficient of the agar-agar mixture to cover the decoration and leave for 2-3 minutes to set.

6. Cover with the tofu which has been simmered for 10 minutes and then cut into dice. Cover with the remainder of the agar-agar mixture and leave to set.

7. Turn out and cut into 3 inch (7.5cm) squares.

CELERY, WILD RICE AND PECAN RING

½ lb (225g) fresh sliced blanched celery
¾ lb (340g) cooked wild rice or long
grain brown rice
3 oz (85g) ground pecans or walnuts
3 oz (85g) spring onions, finely sliced
2 tablespoons finely sliced parsley
Pinch of sea salt

1. Combine all ingredients and press into a moistened ring mould.

2. Taste, and add seasonings if required.

3. Chill and turn out.

4. Fill the centre with shredded lettuce, watercress leaves, grated carrot, grated radish slices and cucumber twists.

MIXED GRAIN SALAD

Combine 6 oz (170g) cooked brown rice with 1 or more of the following:

3 oz (85g) cooked barley, rye or oats
3 oz (85g) cooked millet or buckwheat
2 oz (55g) bean sprouts or seed sprouts
2 oz (55g) lightly cooked green beans or
broad beans
2 oz (55g) lightly toasted chopped nuts
or seeds
2 oz (55g) celery, chopped or carrot,
grated
Mustard cress or watercress to garnish
1 tablespoon oil
2-3 tablespoons vinegar

1. Combine the grains, sprouts, vegetables, nuts or seeds, as selected, in a bowl.

2. Combine the oil and vinegar to make a dressing. (Try apple cider or brown rice vinegar.)

3. When serving salads, it is better to serve the dressing in a separate bowl to allow for individual tastes.

BROWN RICE SALAD

1 lb (455g) cooked brown rice
4 oz (110g) diced, cooked carrot
4 oz (110g) fresh peas
¾ lb (340g) Chinese leaves, finely shredded
2 oz (55g) red pepper, blanched (optional)
Squeeze of lemon juice, or 2-3 teaspoons apple cider vinegar
Tamari/shoyu soya sauce to taste

1. Combine all the ingredients.

2. Season lightly according to taste.

RICE SALAD TRIANGLES

1 lb (455g) cooked brown rice
Green peas, blanched
Sweetcorn, blanched
Carrot, diced and blanched

1. Form the rice into a mound on a flat plate, and mark into three sections.

2. Cover one section with green peas, one with sweetcorn and the third with diced carrot. This gives an attractive layout.

3. Either the rice or the vegetables can be pre-tossed in a salad dressing of your choice.

BEAN SALAD

½ lb (225g) cooked kidney beans
6 oz (170g) cooked green beans, cut in 1 inch (2.5cm) strips
4 oz (110g) Chinese leaves, shredded
1 tablespoon parsley, finely chopped

Dressing 1:
1 tablespoon oil
1-2 umeboshi plums, stoned
2 spring onions, finely sliced
1 tablespoon tamari/shoyu soya sauce

Dressing 2:
1 tablespoon apple cider vinegar
1 tablespoon oil
Pinch of mixed herbs

1. Combine the kidney beans and green beans and add the Chinese leaves and parsley.

2. To make dressing 1, heat the oil and then blend all the dressing ingredients, mixing well.

3. For dressing 2, blend all ingredients.

4. Pour the dressing over the salad and toss to mix. This dish keeps well in a refrigerator for 1-3 days.

Gorgeous Garnishes and Attractive Accompaniments

A garnish should both look good and taste good, and not merely be an inedible decoration. The flavour of a garnish should either be a delicate complement or a refreshing contrast to the accompanying dish. The contrast of texture and colour of a well-chosen garnish can make all the difference between a nourishing but plain meal and an equally nourishing but attractive dish.

Always use best quality ingredients for the best results. Examples of garnishes include:

Fresh herbs, for example, parsley, chives or fennel.

Attractively sliced raw or blanched vegetables, for example, carrot and radish flowers, carrot and turnip matchsticks, watercress, cauliflower and broccoli sprigs, slope-cut celery and fennel, cucumber cubes, slivers and triangles, the green and white of finely cut spring onions, sautéed mushrooms and onion rings, diced red and green peppers (always blanched) and finely sliced rounds of home-grown tomatoes.

Toasted flaked or whole nuts and seeds, such as almonds, hazelnuts, sunflower, sesame and pumpkin seeds, walnuts, pecans and pistachio nuts.

Bean and seed sprouts, such as alfalfa, mung and aduki beans.

Assorted garnishes such as lemon wedges, finely sliced dulse, shrimps and prawns, a swirl of natural yogurt or a grating of cheese.

CROÛTONS

1-2 tablespoons oil
2 slices wholegrain bread, cut into dice

1. Heat the oil in a shallow pan and add the diced bread.

2. Toss in the oil over a medium heat and when crisp and golden, remove from the pan.

3. Drain on absorbent paper, and serve hot.

Herb croûtons

For extra flavour, add a pinch of dried herbs or finely sliced garlic clove to the oil, or sprinkle the fried croûtons with finely chopped fresh herbs such as parsley, chives or thyme.
Serve with soups, or in place of a savoury crumble as a topping for pulse casseroles.

Toasted croûtons

Lightly toast a slice of bread, then cut into dice.

Cheese croûtons

Toast the bread on one side only, and spread the other with cream cheese, cottage cheese or crowdie and top with a finely grated white Cheddar, Cheshire or blue cheese. Toast under the grill and slice into thin strips. This is especially good with onion or leek soup.

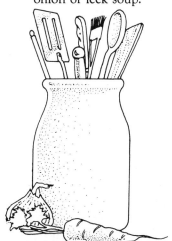

POTATO CROÛTONS

½ lb (225g) potatoes
2-3 tablespoons oil for shallow frying

1. Scrub the potatoes (peeling is optional), and cut into dice.

2. Soak in cold water for 20 minutes, drain, and dry on absorbent paper or cloth.

3. Blanch for 2-3 minutes in boiling water, drain, dry slightly and shallow fry in oil until golden brown. Herbs may be added during cooking.

4. Lift out and serve hot, sprinkled lightly with sea salt.

VEGETABLE PIROSHSKI

These are the Russian equivalent of Cornish pasties, tiny pastry cases, made from rye, barley or organically grown wholewheat flour, filled with cooked vegetables, wholegrains and pulses, baked and served with a winter vegetable soup.

4 oz (110g) pastry (p. 107)
6 oz (170g) cooked vegetables,
wholegrains or pulses

1. Roll out the pastry and use the rim of a teacup or coffee cup to cut out suitable sized rounds for the piroshski.

2. Put on the filling, fold over and seal.

3. Bake at 425°F/220°C/gas mark 7, for 5 minutes or until golden.

Note: Other suitable accompaniments for soups and salads are tiny rolls of bean or lentil pâté tossed in sesame seeds, millet squares (cold, sliced, cooked millet) and miniature rice balls.

PICKLES

Pickles are a naturally fermented food which aids the digestion of grains and can take the place of sweet foods to balance a meal. Where digestion is poor, it is best to avoid ingredients such as vinegar, spices and sugar, as well as commercial pickles containing artificial flavourings, colourings and preservatives.

There is a wide variety of pickling methods, but the following recipes choose the simplest. If the taste is too salty, soak the pickles in cold water for 20-30 minutes before serving.

DILL PICKLES

2 oz (55g) sea salt
2 pints (1.1 litres) water
2 lb (900g) cucumber, cauliflower, broccoli or carrots
1 medium onion
1 teaspoon dill seed, or 1-2 sprigs of fresh dill

1. Bring the salt and water to the boil, simmer for 3 minutes and then cool.

2. Wash and slice the cucumber and onion and place in a large glass or stoneware jar with the dill.

3. Cover with the salted water, making sure that there are no vegetables above the water.

4. Place in a cool, dark place for 3-4 days covered with a piece of muslin cloth to keep dust-free. After this time, cover with a lid, refrigerate, and use within three weeks.

SAUERKRAUT

2½ lb (1.12 kg) white cabbage
2 oz (55g) sea salt

1. Wash and finely slice the cabbage.

2. Place in a glass bowl or a stoneware jar, sprinkle with the salt, and mix well to produce juice from the cabbage.

3. Press the cabbage down into a jar or other container with a plate and a heavy weight. The plate should be slightly smaller than the circumference of the container.

4. Cover with a muslin-type cloth and place in a cool dark place. After 24 hours, the pressed liquid should completely cover the cabbage. If not, add more weights or top up with a little brine solution (1 tablespoon sea salt to 8 fl oz [225ml] water).

5. Leave for 2 weeks, but check the container every day, removing any mould which may form.

6. When ready, rinse and store in the refrigerator. Serve as a crunchy condiment.

Note: 1 tablespoon juniper berries makes a flavoursome addition to the cabbage.

CUCUMBER, RADISH AND ONION PICKLE

10 inch (25cm) cucumber, finely sliced
1 medium onion or 4-6 spring onions,
finely sliced
6 oz (170g) radishes, thinly sliced
Sea salt

1. Lightly salt each ingredient separately and press for 2 hours. Do this by placing the vegetables in a bowl, covering with a plate or saucer, and applying pressure using metal weights, or a jar of beans or rice.

2. After 2 hours, rinse off the salt and combine the ingredients. This makes a light pickle which can be served as a garnish for grain and pulse dishes.

RADISH FLOWERS

Remove the radish tops and roots, and then cut the radishes into flowers. There are two possible cutting styles.

1. Make zig-zag cuts around the centre of each radish and pull the two sections apart.

2. Stand the radish on its base, wedged between two chopsticks. Slice through the radish at right angles to the chopsticks. Rotate the radish 90° and repeat the slicing. This makes 4 petals.

Once cut, blanch the flowers in umeboshi vinegar (p. 84) and water for 2-3 minutes and allow to cool. If using raw, sit the flowers made by cutting style (2) in cold water to allow the 'petals' to open. The radish flowers make an attractive garnish.

FANTASTIC FLAVOURINGS AND DELICIOUS DRESSINGS

Herbs are the basis of an almost endless variety of delicious flavourings. The value of herbs is best appreciated when they are correctly chosen for the food whose flavour and digestibility you wish to enhance, and when used in balanced and suitable proportions. Fresh and dried herbs have been included as optional ingredients in a number of recipes where their use has been found to be appropriate.

HERBAL HINTS

Dried herbs are more concentrated in flavour than fresh herbs, so use sparingly. Buy them in small quantities and store in airtight containers. One quarter of a teaspoon of dried herbs will flavour 1 lb (455g) of fish, ½ lb (225g) of meat or two cups of sauce or vegetables.

Crush dried herbs in the palm of your hand before adding, to help hasten the release of the flavour. In dishes such as stews and casseroles, add dried herbs during the last half hour of cooking and/or fresh herbs, freshly chopped, in the last 10 minutes of cooking, or as a garnish just before serving.

When combining herbs, use those whose flavours are complementary, for example:
green anise and cardamoms with apples,
marjoram, thyme and parsley with a root
vegetable casserole,

tarragon and dill seed with a seasonal salad.

Every garden is large enough to support a corner devoted to growing herbs. Choose an easily accessible, sheltered and sunny location. Those without a garden can keep a year-round supply of fresh herbs in a window box, or indoors in flower pots.

Start off your collection of dried herbs and herb plants with a selection of those which are most commonly used. These include bay leaf, thyme, parsley, sage, fennel, dill, garlic, marjoram, oregano, basil, green anise and cardamom.

Bouquet garni
To make a bouquet garni, you require a 4 inch (10cm) square of muslin or similar fine cotton cloth, and an 8 inch (20cm) piece of cotton thread. You also require:
1 small bay leaf
3-4 stems of parsley (the stem or stalk has more flavour than the leaf)
1 sprig of thyme
Put the herbs in the centre of the muslin, collect the cloth together to form a bag and tie with the thread. Add to soups and casseroles during cooking and remove prior to serving.

The following flavouring and seasoning agents also appear in the recipes in this book:

1. *Allspice.* Also known as Jamaica pepper. Mild and spicy, it is used for pickling and for spicing pies, casseroles etc.

2. *Bonito dried fish flakes*: Wafer-thin shavings of steamed, dried, wood-smoked mackerel, used in small amounts to flavour soup stocks, sauces and tofu (soya bean curd).

3. *Brown rice vinegar*: Made by fermenting brown rice in wooden kegs for two years. It is ideal for dressing summer salads.

4. *Cayenne pepper*: Ground from red chilli peppers, this is very hot and spicy. It is not recommended for regular use.

5. *Cinnamon.* This is available in the powdered form, or as cinnamon sticks. It is particularly good in apple dishes, cakes, puddings and mulled wine.

6. *Cloves*: Pungent and aromatic, these can be used sparingly with apples and in bread sauces and stuffings. They can be bought whole or ground. Ground cloves can be used with other spices in fruit cakes and in mince pie mixtures.

7. *Curry powder*: Use sparingly, or make your own using a mixture of cumin, turmeric, coriander, fenugreek and red pepper, finely ground together. Proportions vary depending on the hotness of the curry desired.

8. *Garlic*: Present and recent meat eaters, and cheese and milk consumers appear to benefit from the use of garlic. Long-term grain, pulse and vegetable eaters tend to prefer the more subtle effect of raw spring onions or cooked onions with only sparing use of garlic, if used at all.

9. *Ginger*: Available as the fresh root, or in dried form. The grated, squeezed root is used to aid the digestion of brassicas (Brussels sprouts, cabbages, etc.) and in dips and sauces to accompany deep-fried foods. Use dried ginger in cakes and biscuits, and crystallized ginger in stuffings, sweet sauces and as a garnish.

10. *Herbs*: (p. 82).

11. *Horseradish*: The fresh, raw root is used finely grated as a digestive aid and is especially good with red meat and fish dishes. It is attributed with many medicinal properties and although these are lost when it is cooked, it is worth using for the flavour alone.

12. *Juniper berries*: The dried berries may be crushed and added to savoury or sweet apple dishes or used whole in marinades, in cabbage pickle (sauerkraut) and with game.

13. *Miso*: (See p. 23).

14. *Mixed spice*: A mixture of cinnamon, allspice, coriander, nutmeg and cloves, this enhances the flavour of apple dishes, cakes and puddings.

15. *Mustard*: This is best used in moderation in the whole or crushed seed form. Although this condiment blends well with pulse, vegetable and grain dishes, it is best used with red meats to aid their digestion.

16. *Nutmeg*: This is the highly aromatic kernel of the fruit of a small tree. Buy the whole kernels and grate as required. Use *very* sparingly. It brings out the flavour of mushrooms.

17. *Paprika*: This is a powder ground from sweet red peppers or pimentos. It is used traditionally in Hungarian cookery and has a spicy, mildly hot flavour.

18. *Pepper*: If using pepper, the pure ground white or black pepper is recommended, the black having a stronger, spicier flavour than the white. Spices tend to complement animal foods better than vegetable dishes.

19. *Saffron*: This is made from the yellow stamens of a crocus flower. Understandably very expensive, it is used in minute quantities only to give a delicate flavour and colour to bland foods such as rice.

20. *Sea salt*: This contains a wide range of minerals and trace elements, unlike regular

table salt which comprises refined sodium chloride and a variety of additional substances such as magnesium carbonate or yellow prussate of soda, included by the manufacturer to help it to flow easily from the salt cellar. Sea salt may be purchased fine, medium or coarse ground. It is recommended to make sparing use of salt and all salt-flavoured seasonings.

21. *Seaweeds and seaweed powders*: These are a useful and well-balanced source of vitamins, minerals and trace elements. Available in dried form.

22. *Sesame salt or gomasio*: Roasted, whole sesame seeds ground with roasted sea salt. Generally bought made up in a ratio of 12 parts seeds to 1 part salt.

23. *Shitake mushrooms*: These are a useful store-cupboard ingredient, prized for their subtle flavour and highly regarded in Japanese medicinal cooking. Use in soups and casseroles.

24. *Soya sauce*: Traditional varieties are available under the names shoyu and tamari. Both are made from soya beans and sea salt. Shoyu has the addition of wheat and has a rich flavour resulting from a long fermentation process. Both are very salty, so use sparingly in cooked dishes. Avoid adding at the table.

25. *Tahini*: A creamy spread prepared from whole or dehusked sesame seeds.

26. *Tekka*: A very strongly flavoured table seasoning for vegetable and grain dishes. It is made by finely chopping and roasting carrots, burdock, lotus root and fresh ginger root, and mixing these ingredients with hatcho miso and unrefined sesame oil in an iron pot for several hours until very dark. Use sparingly on cold winter days.

27. *Tofu*: A high protein, low-fat curd made from soya beans.

28. *Umeboshi plums*: Japanese plums, which are harvested green and pickled in brine (sea salt and water). Shiso leaves, also known as beef steak leaves, are added to give the characteristic pink colour which results after 12-18 months pickling. Rich in enzymes and lactic acid, umeboshi plums act as a digestive aid and are mildly laxative to those with chronic constipation – chew well ⅓-½ an umeboshi before main meals, i.e. 3 times a day, for 5-7 days, and thereafter only as required. High in salt, umeboshis can be soaked in water for 1-2 hours prior to use. Use the soaking water for seasoning vegetables.

29. *Ume vinegar*: An umeboshi plum soaked in water will give a light, balanced vinegar which is well tolerated. It is useful in salad dressings. A little umeboshi paste can be used to preserve cooked rice, as in rice balls or sushi, for travelling or packed lunches.

30. *Vanilla essence*: Always buy the best quality, genuine essence, not the artificial flavouring. It is expensive, but is used in minute amounts.

31. *Vanilla pod*: Choose those covered with white crystals as this indicates freshness. Keep in an airtight jar with soft brown sugar which will become flavoured with the vanilla. When using, halve the pod, scrape out the seeds, and add both pod and seeds to the liquid. When the liquid is well flavoured, remove the pod, dip in warm water to rinse, dry and return to the sugar jar.

32. *Vinegar*: Those recommended include ume vinegar, apple cider vinegar and brown rice vinegar.

33. *Yeast extract*: Various brand names are available. These products contain a mixture of ingredients, including vegetables, sea vegetables and herbs. Wheat-free and artificial additive-free, these seasonings are preferable to most stock cubes and take the place of bone stock.

APPLE AND RAISIN CHUTNEY I

2 lb (900g) sweet eating apples, e.g. Cox's
Orange Pippins
2 fl oz (55ml) unsweetened apple juice
2 oz (55g) chopped walnuts
5 oz (140g) raisins
2 fl oz (55ml) apple cider vinegar
Special herbs for apple pies (cinnamon,
citrus peel, fennel, cardamom seeds,
clove)

1. Core, but do not peel, the apples and cut
into dice.

2. Put all the ingredients into a heavy pan,
stir well and simmer with the lid on until
tender.

3. Remove the lid and simmer, stirring
frequently, until the chutney is thick.

4. Store the chutney in glass jars or stoneware
containers with well-fitting lids (vinegar will
corrode metal lids). Put the clean jars into a
very slow oven to dry and warm, 225°F/
100°C/gas mark ¼. Fill the warm jars with
the hot chutney and put the lids on at once.

5. Label and date the chutney, and store in a
cool, dark place, or the refrigerator. Do not
keep for longer than 1 week because of the
low vinegar and sugar content.

APPLE AND RAISIN CHUTNEY II

4 lb (1.8kg) sweet apples
1 lb (455g) seedless raisins or sultanas
½ lb (225g) chopped nuts
Pinch of ground cloves
½ pint (280ml) brown rice or apple cider
vinegar
1 lb (455g) soft brown sugar (optional)
2 oranges

1. Peel, core and chop the apples.

2. Place the apples, raisins, nuts, spice and
vinegar in a covered pot and simmer until
soft and thoroughly cooked.

3. Add the sugar, and the juice and rind of
the oranges, and cook, uncovered, until
thick, stirring at least until the sugar is
dissolved.

4. Store in jars as described above. This
chutney will keep well in a cool, dark
cupboard for several months if sugar is used.

APRICOT CHUTNEY

1 lb (455g) dried apricots
3 cloves garlic
1 teaspoon sea salt
½ lb (225g) preserved ginger
2 lb (900g) dates
1 lb (455g) sultanas
1 lb (455g) soft brown sugar
Apple cider vinegar
Walnuts (optional)

1. Soak the apricots.

2. Crush the garlic with a teaspoon of sea
salt.

3. Chop the ginger.

4. Cook all ingredients together until the
flavours are blended. This takes about two
hours.

5. Store in jars as described in Apple and
Raisin Chutney I.

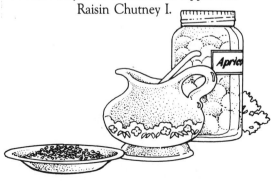

CHESTNUT STUFFING

**1 lb (455g) fresh chestnuts, ½ lb (225g)
dried chestnuts or 1 tin chestnut purée
Little sea salt
1 large onion, finely chopped
¾ lb (340g) finely grated carrot (optional)
½ lb (225g) rye breadcrumbs or oatflakes
Vegetable stock to mix, if necessary**

1. If using dried chestnuts, soak overnight, then simmer with a pinch of sea salt for 30-40 minutes, until cooked.

2. Drain, then pound or purée the chestnuts and mix all the ingredients together to form a stiff paste.

3. Use to stuff the fowl. This stuffing is particularly delicious with turkey. Alternatively, steam in a covered bowl for 45 minutes-1 hour, and serve with a light miso gravy, boiled Brussels sprouts, crunchy pressed salad and a garnish of toasted sunflower seeds.

FRUIT STUFFING

**1 lb (455g) dried apricots or prunes,
soaked and chopped
4 oz (110g) almonds or hazelnuts, toasted
and flaked or chopped
2 small onions, finely chopped
½ lb (225g) rye breadcrumbs or oatflakes,
or cooked brown rice
¼ teaspoon mixed spice
½ teaspoon green anise
1 oz (28g) crystallized ginger, chopped
Soaking water from the fruit to bind**

1. Mix the ingredients together, using enough of the soaking water from the fruit to bind.

2. Either put into a bowl, cover with greaseproof paper and steam for 1-1½ hours, or use to stuff a free-range roasting fowl.

KINLOCH HAGGIS

This recipe is also delicious as a poultry stuffing.

**1 large onion
1 lb (455g) oatflakes
1 teaspoon mixed dried herbs
½ pint (280ml) well flavoured and
seasoned vegetable stock**

1. Finely chop the onion, add the oatflakes and herbs, and mix to a moist but not sloppy consistency with the vegetable stock. This will require more or less stock, depending on the absorbency of the oatflakes.

2. Put into a basin, cover and steam for 1 hour. Turn out and serve.

DULSE AND SCALLIONS

**2 oz (55g) dry weight dulse
1-2 teaspoons sesame oil
6 spring onions (scallions)
1-2 tablespoons tamari/shoyu soya sauce**

1. Rinse the dulse, removing any bits of shell or stone. Soak, just covered in water, for a few minutes.

2. Heat a heavy pan and brush with oil. Add 3 of the onions, finely sliced lengthwise, and sauté for 1 minute.

3. Add the dulse, stir for a few minutes, and then pour on the soaking water. Cover and simmer for 5 minutes.

4. Add tamari/shoyu sauce to taste and simmer for a further 3 minutes.

5. Strain and reserve the liquid for stock. Toss the dulse in a serving bowl with the remaining sliced spring onions.

6. Parsley and toasted sesame seeds can be added if liked, or served as a side dish accompaniment.

NORI CONDIMENT

½ packet (1 oz/28g) shredded or sheet
nori
¼ pint (140ml) water
1-2 tablespoons tamari/shoyu soya sauce

1. Rehydrate the nori in the water, and
simmer for 10 minutes.

2. Add the tamari or shoyu and simmer for a
further 10 minutes without a lid on the pot,
to reduce the liquid, and to blend the
flavours.

3. Serve hot or cold in 1-2 teaspoon
portions with brown rice, millet, fish or
vegetables.

Nori condiment with ginger
Add the freshly pressed juice of a 1 inch
(2.5cm) piece of ginger root to the above
recipe during cooking, and serve with stir-
fry or deep-fry dishes, to aid the digestion of
oily food.

TOFU DIP

½ lb (225g) block of tofu (a low-fat,
high-protein, soya bean product)
Pinch of sea salt, or 2 teaspoons tamari/
shoyu soya sauce
2 tablespoons water
3 tablespoons brown rice vinegar or
apple cider vinegar
2½ tablespoons tahini
1 spring onion, finely sliced

1. Blend all the ingredients until creamy.

Note: All spreads and dips will keep for 2-3
days in a covered container in the refrigerator.

SWEETCORN DIP

2 onions, finely sliced
Pinch of sea salt
2 teaspoons oil
¾ lb (340g) grated carrot
¾ lb (340g) unsweetened sweetcorn
kernels

1. Lightly shallow-fry the onions with the
pinch of sea salt in the oil.

2. Stir in the grated carrot and the sweetcorn
kernels.

3. Cook gently for 15 minutes, until tender,
then blend or sieve the vegetables to produce
a smooth sweet-flavoured dip.

AVOCADO DIP

2 large avocado pears
10 oz (280g) tofu
Juice of half a lemon
Pinch of sea salt and freshly ground
black pepper
Fresh chopped chives

1. Halve the avocados lengthways and
remove the stones.

2. Scoop out the flesh and blend or liquidize
with the tofu, lemon juice and seasonings to
taste.

3. Turn into a serving dish and garnish with
chives.

4. Chill, and serve with toast and/or strips of
raw vegetables.

TOFU DRESSING

½ lb (225g) block of tofu
3 spring onions
3-4 teaspoons umeboshi plum paste
Little water

1. Bring ½ pint (280ml) water to the boil and boil the tofu for 7 minutes. Drain and cool quickly.

2. Dice the spring onions, put about half of them into a suribachi (scored mortar and pestle) or liquidizer, and blend thoroughly.

3. Add the umeboshi paste and the tofu and mash with a little water to a smooth, creamy consistency.

MISO DRESSING

1 tablespoon miso
6 fl oz (170ml) hot water
4 oz (110g) roasted almonds, hazelnuts or walnuts, flaked or finely chopped

1. Blend the miso in the hot water and add the nuts.

2. Use sparingly as a dressing for blanched or pressed salads.

FRENCH DRESSING

2 tablespoons lemon juice
1 tablespoon oil
Pinch of sea salt
Herbs as available, e.g. dill, parsley, chives

1. Whisk the lemon juice into the oil to mix well, or shake together in a well-sealed jar or bottle.

2. Add seasoning and herbs to taste and shake again or whisk prior to use. Use sparingly.

Note: Always serve green salads without dressing and allow guests to add their own. This keeps the leafy ingredients fresh and crisp.

UMEBOSHI PLUM DRESSINGS

Dressing 1:
1 umeboshi plum (remove and keep the stone)
2 tablespoons brown rice vinegar and 1 tablespoon water
2 tablespoons apple juice (optional)
1 tablespoon fresh parsley, chives or spring onions, finely chopped
4 inch (10cm) cucumber, peeled
2 teaspoons oil

1. Blend all the ingredients thoroughly. This recipe is excellent for party use.

Dressing 2
2 umeboshi plums
8 fl oz (225ml) water
1 teaspoon tamari/shoyu soya sauce (optional)

1. Soak the umeboshi plums, with the stones in, for 20 minutes.

2. Remove the stones and strain the juice to remove the pulp.

3. Mix with tamari or shoyu soya sauce. This dressing aids the digestion of raw vegetables, and can be used in place of vinegar.

Dressing 3

2 tablespoons spring onions, chopped
6 fl oz (170ml) water
2 teaspoons tahini
1 tablespoon lemon juice
2 umeboshi plums, without stones

1. Blend all the ingredients thoroughly. Delicious over lightly cooked cauliflower sprigs.

2. By replacing the tahini with 2 teaspoons oil, this makes a good dressing for tossing green salads.

CREAMY SESAME SALAD DRESSING

3 tablespoons tahini
2 tablespoons sesame oil
2 tablespoons lemon juice
¼ teaspoon sea salt
1 teaspoon fresh salad herbs (e.g. chives, parsley, salad burnet, summer savory, marjoram or thyme)
1 clove crushed garlic (optional)
3 tablespoons water

1. Mix the tahini firstly with the oil and then with the lemon juice.

2. Add the salt, the herbs and the garlic, if used, and mix again.

3. Add the water a few drops at a time and blend well until smooth.

TAMARI GRAVY

1 medium onion, chopped
1 teaspoon oil
2 tablespoons arrowroot/kuzu
1 pint (570ml) vegetable stock
1 dessertspoon tomato purée (optional)
1 dessertspoon tamari/shoyu soya sauce

1. Lightly sauté the onion in the oil.

2. Dissolve the arrowroot in a little cold water and add to the onions.

3. Stir in the vegetable stock, mixing to a smooth consistency.

4. Stir in the other ingredients and allow to simmer and thicken before serving.

ARROWROOT/KUZU SAUCE OR GRAVY

½ pint (280ml) vegetable or kombu stock
Sea salt, tamari/shoyu soya sauce, or yeast extract to flavour
1-2 teaspoons ginger juice (optional)
1 tablespoon arrowroot/kuzu

1. Put the liquid into a small pot, heat and flavour to taste.

2. Dissolve the arrowroot in 2 teaspoons cold water and stir into the heated liquid.

3. Turn up the heat and continue stirring until the mixture turns from cloudy to clear.

TAMARI/SHOYU AND GINGER SAUCE

This sauce is delicious poured over blanched cabbage, other leafy green vegetables, carrots or boiled brown rice.

1 onion, finely chopped
2 teaspoons sesame oil
8 fl oz (225ml) water
1 teaspoon fresh ginger root
Little tamari/shoyu soya sauce to flavour
2 teaspoons arrowroot/kuzu

1. Sauté the onion in the oil.

2. Add the water and the crushed ginger root and simmer gently for a few minutes.

3. Add tamari to taste.

4. Dissolve the kuzu in a little cold water and stir into the sauce, using a wooden spoon.

TAHINI MISO SAUCE

1 lb (455g) vegetables of choice
(cauliflower, carrot, leek, broccoli etc.)
6 fl oz (170ml) vegetable stock or water
2 tablespoons miso
1 tablespoon tahini

1. Lightly steam or boil the vegetables.

2. Drain the unsalted cooking stock and make up to 6 fl oz (170ml) with water or kombu stock.

3. Blend in the miso and tahini and mix to a smooth paste.

4. Serve over the vegetables and garnish with freshly chopped parsley, spring onion, or ½ teaspoon grated lemon rind.

TRANSITION WHITE/ BÉCHAMEL/CREAM SAUCE

2 tablespoons oil
2 tablespoons barley flour
½ pint (280ml) soya milk, cow's milk or
vegetable/kombu stock
1-2 teaspoons miso or yeast extract or
¼ teaspoon sea salt
1 tablespoon freshly chopped parsley

1. Heat the oil and add the flour, stirring constantly over a medium to low heat, until the flour forms a smooth roux or pastry ball.

2. Gradually stir in half the milk or stock, then add the seasoning and finally the remainder of the milk or stock, stirring continually to prevent lumps, until the mixture is smooth and thickened.

3. Stir in the parsley and serve over vegetables or as an optional extra.

4. For a brown sauce, slightly toast the flour until golden. This brings out the flavour and gives a nutty taste.

GLUTEN-FREE BÉCHAMEL SAUCE

½ pint (280ml) vegetable or kombu
stock, water, cow's milk or soya milk
1-2 teaspoons miso or yeast extract
2 tablespoons maize meal, arrowroot or
kuzu thickener, dissolved in 1½
tablespoons cold water

1. Combine the stock or milk with the seasoning in a pot.

2. Heat to simmering, stir in the dissolved thickener and cook for 1-2 minutes until thickened and the mixture turns from cloudy to clear.

3. Serve as above. This is a lighter textured version than the flour sauce.

Variations for Béchamel Sauce

Herb sauce: In place of parsley, try fresh or dried basil, thyme, sage, oregano, marjoram.
Mushroom sauce: Start by sautéing 4 oz (110g) mushrooms, then add the flour, or add the sautéed mushrooms prior to adding the arrowroot. A tiny pinch of nutmeg brings out the flavour in mushroom dishes.
Tahini sauce: Add 1 tablespoon sesame tahini after the sauce is thickened.
Ginger sauce: Add 1-2 teaspoons ginger juice with miso. This is especially good with boiled greens.

CAULIFLOWER SAUCE

This is delicious served with cooked brown rice, brown lentils, carrots and spring greens.

1 lb (455g) cauliflower florets
¼ pint (140ml) kombu stock
¼ pint (140ml) sesame tahini
Tamari/shoyu soya sauce to taste

1. Simmer the cauliflower florets in the stock until tender, and then sieve or liquidize.

2. Blend with the tahini.

3. Reheat thoroughly and season to taste with the soya sauce.

TREMENDOUSLY TROPICAL SAUCE

For very special summer occasions.

1 ripe banana
1 teaspoon sesame oil
2 teaspoons honey
1 teaspoon miso or yeast extract
1 sweet apple, grated
1 tablespoon apple cider or brown rice vinegar
2 teaspoons fresh grated ginger juice or 1 teaspoon powdered ginger
Tamari/shoyu soya sauce to taste

1. Slice the banana and lightly fry in the oil.

2. Blend in the honey and the miso, then add the apple, vinegar and ginger.

3. Simmer over a very low heat for 3-5 minutes to blend the flavours.

4. Taste and adjust seasoning as required.

5. Serve hot or cold with plain boiled rice and lightly steamed greens, e.g. cabbage, Chinese leaves, broccoli, cauliflower, etc.

BROWN LENTIL SAUCE

This sauce is good with buckwheat or millet and lightly cooked greens.

1½ lb (670g) cooked brown lentils (p. 37)
¼ pint (140ml) lentil stock
1 tablespoon arrowroot or kuzu, dissolved in 1 tablespoon cold water

1. Sieve or blend the lentils with the stock.

2. Reheat and thicken with the arrowroot or kuzu.

BEAN SAUCE

½ lb (225g) cooked beans, peas, lentils
or chick peas (p. 37)
¼ pint (140ml) bean stock
2 tablespoons tahini (optional)
1 clove garlic (optional)
1 tablespoon tamari/shoyu soya sauce or
1-2 teaspoons miso or yeast extract
1 tablespoon lemon juice
3 tablespoons chopped parsley

1. Combine the cooked beans and the stock
in a blender (or suribachi) with the tahini
and garlic.

2. Taste and add the seasonings and the
lemon juice.

3. Serve reheated and sprinkled with parsley,
or serve cold as a dip.

Note: This sauce can also be used as an
instant soup stock. Add fresh or dried
vegetables to a little boiling water in a
covered pot and cook until just tender.
Make up the liquid, depending on the
number of people to be served (¼ pint
[140ml] each), using kombu stock or water
and blend in 1-2 tablespoons bean sauce to
taste.
Serve garnished with watercress, beansprouts
or spring onion.

ADUKI BEAN AND ONION SAUCE

1 onion, finely chopped
2 cloves garlic, crushed (optional)
1 tablespoon oil (optional)
½ lb (225g) cooked aduki beans (p. 37)
Sea salt to taste

1. Simmer or sauté the chopped onion and
the crushed garlic, if used, until tender.

2. Add to the beans, blend or sieve and
season to taste.

3. Serve hot as a sauce with brown rice and
vegetables.

4. Alternatively, simmer for a few minutes
more to thicken and use as a vegetable
spread on brown toast, garnished with
chopped spring onions or parsley.

JUST DESSERTS

The combination of starchy foods (pastry, sponges, bread, potatoes, grains, etc.) with fruit, either fresh or cooked, is too much for some human digestive systems. The result is often flatulence and indigestion.

Other people are less fortunate and can eat such mixtures with no visible signs of distress, apart from the odd stomach rumble. Such people seldom need to practise caution when choosing food, and can, as a result, end up by abusing their bodies.

The following recipes are included for use, if used at all, on those special occasions when a sweet course seems appropriate, such as birthdays, Christmas, and similar celebrations. The recipes range from easy-to-digest fruit jellies to rich-tasting family puddings and elegant ideas for entertaining.

While sugar is avoided as much as possible, where it occurs it is used in its crude, less refined, forms – Muscovado or Barbados sugar, soft brown sugar and crude black molasses. Honey, rice syrup and barley malt are also used as alternatives to white sugar. Contrary to popular belief, it *is* possible to create a soft brown sugar Pavlova cake!

Flour, too, is always used as the whole-meal variety, but in a number of recipes whole flakes are substituted for all or part of the flour. Some people find flakes easier to digest than flour, and flakes do not suffer the same vitamin losses as can occur when grain is ground to flour, with a consequent greater risk of oxidation. These comments about sugar and flour also apply to the 'Wholesome Home Baking' section (p. 103).

When using fruit, where possible, use produce which has been grown organically without the use of artificial fertilizers, herbicides and pesticides. When in doubt, wash the fruit carefully and then peel it. According to your own state of health, the climate and the season, eat fruit fresh and raw or lightly cooked, or use soaked, dried fruit as a sweetener. For proper digestion, fruit is best eaten on its own or combined in a jelly with agar-agar, as this seaweed contains minerals and trace elements which aid digestion. Alternatively, set the fruit in a sauce, thickened with kuzu or arrowroot.

A seasonal salad, a spoonful of sauerkraut or similar non-vinegar pickle, or a wineglass full of vegetable juice, are all excellent alternatives to the traditional dessert or biscuits and cheese, without the drawbacks of the more traditional fare.

The following chapters are designed to make the transition from refined foods to wholefoods an enjoyable experience. If you use only *this* section of the book, you will at least have added variety to your daily diet.

FRESH FRUIT SALAD

A quick and delicious fresh fruit salad may be made by adding freshly peeled and chopped fruit to unsweetened fruit juice. Try the following:

¼ pint (140ml) unsweetened apple juice
1 sprig fresh mint
Juice of ½ fresh lemon
1 apple, peeled and sliced
1 or more portions of fresh fruit in season, e.g.
grapes, black, green or seedless
peach, remove skin, stone and chop
pear, strawberries, raspberries, blackcurrants
1 peeled and pithed orange
1 small banana, sliced

1. Mix all the ingredients well with the juice. This will keep in a cool place for 2-3 hours, but is best used as fresh as possible. The banana should always be added immediately before serving.

2. Try adding 8 fresh mint leaves, 1 teaspoon dried mint or a pinch of green anise to fruit salad and mix well.

VANILLA ICE CREAM

½ pint (280ml) apple juice
2 inch (5cm) piece of vanilla pod
4 beaten eggs
¼ teaspoon sea salt
¼ pint (140ml) sunflower oil
¼ teaspoon cinnamon

1. Mix all the ingredients down to the salt in a pot, heat gently, stirring constantly, and simmer for 5 minutes to thicken.

2. Cool the mixture and remove the vanilla pod.

3. Purée, press through a fine sieve and stir in the sunflower oil and cinnamon. Fruits and nuts can be added if liked.

4. Chill in the freezer compartment until frozen, about 3-4 hours.

FRUIT JUICE JELLIES

1 pint (570ml) unsweetened fruit juice
2 tablespoons agar-agar, powder or flakes

1. Heat the juice in a saucepan and add the agar-agar. (Check the instructions on the packet.)

2. Stir to mix, then pour into a mould and allow to set.

Note: Seasonal soft fruit can be added to the hot juice or, alternatively, arrange the fruit in a serving dish or individual bowls, pour the jelly over, and allow to set.

APRICOT KANTEN OR JELLY

For this recipe use Hunza apricots if you can get them. They are more expensive but delicious.

1 lb (455g) apricots pre-soaked in 1 pint (570ml) water
4 tablespoons agar-agar flakes

1. Boil the apricots in the water, cool, strain off the juice and purée.

2. To 1 pint (570ml) of the apricot juice add the agar-agar flakes and bring to the boil. Simmer for 5 minutes, stirring continually.

3. Add the apricot purée after the mixture begins to cool and leave to set.

FRESH FRUIT KANTEN

1½ lb (670g) fresh fruit, such as plums,
pears, peaches, strawberries, etc.
¾ pint (420ml) unsweetened apple juice
2-3 finely chopped leaves of mint or
lemon balm (optional)
1½ tablespoons arrowroot or kuzu

1. Simmer the halved and de-stoned or
cored fruit for 5 minutes in the apple juice.

2. Remove the fruit to a serving dish or
individual dishes and sprinkle with the
mint.

3. Reheat the juice. Dissolve the arrowroot
or kuzu in a little cold water and add to the
juice. Stir continuously until thickened.
The mixture will change from cloudy to
clear. Pour over the fruit and leave to set.

STRAWBERRY KANTEN

1½ pints (840ml) apple juice
7 tablespoons agar-agar
⅛ teaspoon sea salt
1 tablespoon kuzu
1 lb (455g) strawberries
2 teaspoons tahini (optional)

1. Place the juice, agar-agar and salt in a pot
and bring to the boil.

2. Dissolve the kuzu in a little cold water and
add to the mixture, stirring continuously.

3. Liquidize half of the strawberries and
chop the remainder, reserving some of the
chopped fruit for a garnish. Add the liquidized
fruit to the agar-agar-kuzu mixture with the
tahini and cook gently, stirring continuously
until the mixture thickens. Add the
remaining strawberries.

4. Pour into a large bowl, or individual
glasses, and garnish with the reserved
strawberries.

APPLE AND RAISIN DELIGHT

2 lb (900g) apples (dessert or cooking)
6 oz (170g) raisins
Pinch of cinnamon or mixed spice
(optional)
1 tablespoon water
2 fl oz (55ml) apple concentrate, in ½
pint (280ml) water
2 tablespoons arrowroot/kuzu dissolved
in 2 tablespoons water
1 tablespoon toasted flaked almonds

1. Quarter and core the apples into a
cooking pot, add the raisins and sprinkle
with the spice, if used.

2. Cook gently with the water until tender.

3. Turn into a serving dish.

4. Put the apple concentrate and water into
a pot and add the dissolved arrowroot. Stir
continuously until the mixture thickens,
turning from cloudy to clear.

5. Pour the mixture over the gently cooked
fruit, and allow to set or serve hot. This
tastes delicious garnished with toasted flaked
almonds.

READY-MADE RICH CRUMBLE TOPPING

1 tablespoon oil
1 tablespoon honey, real maple syrup or
brown rice syrup (optional)
½ lb (225g) rolled oat flakes
2 oz (55g) toasted breadcrumbs (optional)
2 oz (55g) mixed toasted chopped
almonds, hazelnuts and sesame seeds
2 oz (55g) toasted sunflower seeds
Pinch of sea salt
2 oz (55g) raisins (optional)

1. Heat the oil with the honey over a
medium heat in a large, shallow, heavy-
based pot.

2. Add the oats and then the breadcrumbs,
stirring well to coat.

3. When golden, add the toasted nuts and
seeds. Continue stirring to blend the flavours.

4. Lastly, add the salt, which aids the
digestion of the grain.

5. Transfer the mixture to a bowl to cool,
mix in the raisins and store in an airtight
glass jar ready for use over lightly-cooked
fresh or dried fruits, or as an energy-giving
snack or breakfast ingredient.

6. By leaving out the sweetener and the
raisins, this can be used as a topping for
savoury dishes, adding 2 oz (55g) finely
grated white cheese if wished.

APPLE AND OATFLAKE CRUMBLE

2 lb (900g) dessert apples*
4 oz (110g) raisins
Pinch of cinnamon
1 tablespoon unsweetened apple
concentrate, diluted in 1 tablespoon
water
½ lb (225g) oat flakes
2 tablespoons whole barley flour or
organically-grown wholewheat flour
Pinch of sea salt
2 tablespoons oil

1. Core and slice the apples, place in a
lightly-oiled baking dish and add the raisins.

2. Mix the cinnamon with the unsweetened
apple juice and pour over the fruit.

3. To make the topping, mix the oat flakes
with the flour and a pinch of sea salt, and
then rub in the oil until the mixture is like
breadcrumbs.

4. Sprinkle over the apples and bake at
350°F/180°C/gas mark 4 until golden
brown, 25-30 minutes.

*Cooking apples may also be used but using
dessert apples reduces the need for additional
sweetness.

APPLE AND DRIED FRUIT DESSERT

4 oz (110g) dried fruit, apricots, sultanas,
etc.
1 lb (455g) cooking or dessert apples
Pinch of cinnamon or mixed spice
(optional)
3½ fl oz (100ml) plain yogurt
2 teaspoons honey
1 egg white, stiffly beaten

1. Soak the dried fruit overnight.

2. Stew the apples and the soaked dried fruit with the spice until tender.

3. Mix the yogurt with the honey and fold in the stiffly beaten egg white.

4. Spread the yogurt mixture on top of the fruit in an ovenproof dish, and bake in a medium hot oven (350°F/180°C/gas mark 4) until the topping is browned, about 20-30 minutes.

Apple, Pear or Peach and Nut Crumble

2 lb (900g) sliced apples, pears or peaches
2 tablespoons arrowroot
3 fl oz (85ml) water
6 oz (170g) oatflakes
4 oz (110g) chopped walnuts
2 oz (55g) flaked almonds
2 oz (55g) sunflower seeds
2 tablespoons rice syrup

1. Place the fruit in the baking dish, combine the water and the arrowroot and pour over the fruit.

2. Dry roast the oats over a medium heat until golden.

3. Put into a bowl, add the nuts and seeds and finally the syrup and mix well.

4. Sprinkle the mix over the fruit, cover and bake at 375°F/190°C/gas mark 5 for 20-25 minutes, then uncover the dish and bake for a further 5-10 minutes until nicely browned.

Apple Crumble

1 lb (455g) cooking apples
3 oz (85g) cooking dates or sultanas
2 tablespoons cold water
4 oz (110g) wholemeal rye or barley flour, or 2 oz (55g) of each
2 oz (55g) butter or 6 tablespoons oil
Pinch of sea salt
Pinch of cinnamon or mixed spice (optional)
1 oz (28g) flaked nuts or seeds

1. Core and dice the apples, chop the dates and simmer together in 1-2 tablespoons water until tender.

2. Mix together the flour, butter or oil, and salt to make the crumble topping.

3. Put the fruit, with the spice, if used, into an ovenproof pie dish, cover with the crumble topping and bake in the oven at 375°F/190°C/gas mark 5 for approximately 25 minutes.

4. Sprinkle with the flaked nuts and cook for a further 5 minutes to toast the nuts. Serve hot or cold, with or without natural yogurt.

Variation: Instead of sprinkling with chopped nuts, 1 oz (28g) of fresh ground almonds or hazelnuts can be included in the crumble mixture.

CHRISTMAS DREAM PUDDING

Make this pudding a day or two before Christmas, as it improves with keeping. It can be reheated by steaming for about ½ hour.

½ lb (225g) whole flakes (rye, oats, barley, mixed)
6 fl oz (170ml) unsweetened, additive-free grape or apple juice
¾ lb (340g) mixed dried fruit (raisins, sultanas, currants, peel, apricots)
2 tablespoons brandy
2 oz (55g) dark muscovado sugar
1 teaspoon mixed spice
1 teaspoon cinnamon
1 egg

1. Soak the grain flakes for 2-3 hours in the grape or apple juice, and soak the dried fruit in the brandy (use enough brandy to moisten all the fruit).

2. Mix the sugar with the spices, then add the fruit in the brandy, and finally stir in the soaked grain flakes.

3. Add the egg and mix well.

4. Put into a Pyrex bowl, cover well with greaseproof paper and steam for 2-3 hours.

5. Serve hot or cold, with or without a sauce (see Custard, p. 101).

BROWN SUGAR PAVLOVA

3 egg whites
Pinch of sea salt
9 oz (255g) soft brown sugar
1 teaspoon vanilla essence

1. Pre-heat the oven to 250°F/120°C/gas mark ½, and arrange a bottom shelf.

2. Beat the egg whites and salt until quite stiff, fold in the sugar with a large metal spoon and finally add the vanilla essence.

3. Draw a dinner-plate sized circle on non-stick baking paper and pile the meringue mixture into the centre of the circle. Smooth the surface and sides, or leave hollow in the centre.

4. Place on the bottom shelf of the oven and bake for 30 minutes.

5. After this time, reduce the heat to 225°F/110°C/gas mark ¼, and leave for a further hour.

6. Allow to cool.

7. Prepare a mixture of fresh fruit and whipped cream (optional) and pile into the centre of the pavlova immediately before serving.

8. Alternatively, use the meringue mixture to make small meringue shells, and serve sandwiched in pairs with fresh whipped cream.

BUCKWHEAT APPLE FRITTERS

4 oz (110g) buckwheat flour
4 oz (110g) rye or barley flour
3 tablespoons oil
¼ teaspoon sea salt
1 egg
1 tablespoon raisins, pre-soaked
Pinch of cinnamon
1½ lb (670g) sliced apple rings

1. Mix all the ingredients except for the apples, into a batter, adding a little water as required.

2. Dip apple slices into the batter and fry in oil until the batter is puffed and slightly brown.

CREAMY RICE PUDDING

¾ lb (340g) cooked short grain brown
rice (p. 37)
1½ pints (840ml) diluted soya milk
½ teaspoon honey (optional)
4 oz (110g) flaked almonds
4 oz (110g) sultanas or raisins

1. Combine all the ingredients and simmer
very slowly for 20-30 minutes until the rice
is creamy.

2. Stir occasionally to prevent sticking.

3. Alternatively, bake in the oven at 350°F/
180°C/gas mark 4 for 1 hour. Serve hot or
cold.

Variation: The same dessert can be made
using apricots or dates instead of sultanas.
Presoak the apricots and use the soaking
juice combined with the soya milk as part of
the cooking liquid. The flaked almonds can
be toasted and sprinkled on the top of the
baked pudding.

THURI'S ICELAND PIE

Designed for active, healthy explorers and
adventurous eaters.

Crumble mix:
6 oz (170g) oatflakes
1 oz (28g) brown rice flour
½ teaspoon sea salt
1 tablespoon cinnamon
2 tablespoons toasted flaked or chopped
nuts (optional)
2 tablespoons corn or sunflower oil
1 egg or 2 tablespoons apple juice

Pie filling:
5-6 eating or cooking apples or pears, cut
into slices
1 tablespoon raisins or sultanas or fresh
berries
2 tablespoons apple juice

Sauce (optional):
2 tablespoons soya flour
1 pint (570ml) apple juice
Vanilla pod (optional)
1 tablespoon kuzu or arrowroot in 2
tablespoons cold water
Squeeze of lemon juice
2 tablespoons oil
Pinch of sea salt

1. Combine all the crumble ingredients to
form a topping and set aside.

2. Place the apples or pears in an ovenproof
dish, and sprinkle with the raisins and apple
juice.

3. Cover with the crumble mix and bake for
30-40 minutes at 350°F/180°C/gas mark 4.

4. To make the sauce, boil the soya flour
with the apple juice in a heavy pot, stirring
to prevent burning.

5. Add the vanilla pod at this stage if liked.
Boil for 3-5 minutes and then remove the
pod and reduce the heat.

6. Dissolve the kuzu or arrowroot in the
cold water, add the lemon juice, and stir
into the pot. Simmer and stir for a further 3
minutes.

7. In a separate pot heat the oil. Transfer the
sauce to a bowl or blender and whisk in the
oil a drop at a time, as though making
mayonnaise.

8. Add a pinch of salt and blend or whisk for
a further minute for a rich, creamy sauce.

9. Serve poured over the pie.

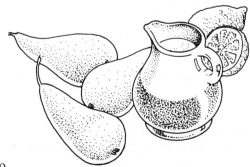

SHEILA'S CHEESECAKE

Base:
3 oz (85g) butter or oil
4 oz (110g) wholegrain flakes (mixed rye, oats and barley)

Filling:
4 oz (110g) cream cheese
4 oz (110g) smooth cottage cheese or Quark
Juice of ½ lemon
2 fl oz (55ml) double cream
1 lb (455g) blackcurrants
Little honey or rice syrup
2 teaspoons arrowroot or kuzu
¼ pint (140ml) double cream (optional)

1. Make the base by melting the butter or oil in a heavy pot and then stirring in the grain flakes.

2. Pour into the bottom of a 9 inch (20cm) flan dish. Press down and allow to set.

3. Beat the cream cheese and the cottage cheese together until well blended, add the lemon juice and mix well.

4. Whip the double cream stiffly and fold into the cheese mixture. Pour over the flake base and allow to set.

5. Meanwhile, gently stew the blackcurrants, sweetening to taste with a little honey or rice syrup.

6. Dissolve the kuzu in a little of the blackcurrant juice, and add to the pot, stirring the mixture until the juice is clear and starting to thicken.

7. Cool and pour over the cheese layer and leave to set.

8. If desired, decorate the top with ¼ pint (140ml) whipped cream.

Variation: For a more digestible alternative, leave out the grain base. Allow half of the blackcurrant mixture to set in the bottom of the flan dish, then cover with the cheese layer, and top with the remainder of the blackcurrants.

Black cherries, or peaches simmered gently in apple juice, can also be used instead of the blackcurrants.

FRUIT JAMS AND BUTTERS

Make these jams in small batches only as they do not keep for long.

FRUIT JAM

Apples, pears and yellow plums make a delicious jam combination.

1. Wash and stone the fruits and put in a pot with half their weight of soft brown sugar.

2. Slowly bring to the boil and simmer to thicken. Pour into pre-heated glass jars and cover.

FRUIT BUTTERS

Apples cooked very slowly over a long period in a little water, with occasional stirring, reducing the liquid by one-third, make a good apple butter.
Plums, blackberries, etc. do not require added water.

Strawberry Kuzu Jam

2 lb (900g) fresh strawberries
2 tablespoons kuzu dissolved in
2 tablespoons cold water
Pinch of sea salt

1. Cook half the strawberries with the kuzu and salt to make a thick sauce.

2. Place the remaining strawberries, whole and raw, in Kilner jars and pour the sauce over them.

3. Pressure cook for one minute with the tops loosely on the jars. When you open the pressure cooker, screw down the lids. Unopened, this 'jam' will keep for a year, but once opened, will only keep 4 days.

Poached Whole Fruits

Peaches, apples, pears, and bananas make a naturally sweet dessert when poached in a little apple juice in the oven for 15 minutes at 375°F/190°C/gas mark 5, or in a covered pot over a medium heat for 10 minutes. Remove the fruit to a serving dish, thicken the juice with arrowroot or kuzu and use as a glaze, serving hot or cold, garnished with toasted flaked almonds.

Carob Sauce

4 tablespoons arrowroot or 2 tablespoons
kuzu
1 tablespoon carob powder
1½ pints (850ml) water
3 fl oz (85ml) concentrated apple juice
Pinch of ground ginger

1. Dissolve the arrowroot or kuzu with the carob in a little of the water. Add to the remaining water, apple juice and ginger in a pot and bring to the boil.

2. Simmer very gently for 20 minutes. If the temperature is too high, the carob can taste powdery.

3. Allow the sauce to cool. Use to pour over baked pears, apples, etc.

Oat Custard

½ lb (225g) whole oats
2 pints (1.1 litres) water
¼ teaspoon sea salt
1 vanilla pod, slit down one side to
release the flavour
1 teaspoon honey
1 teaspoon almond butter
2 teaspoons arrowroot or kuzu, dissolved
in a little water

1. Wash the oats and cook in the water with the salt and vanilla pod for 40 minutes in the pressure cooker, or 1 hour without pressure.

2. Cool and strain, and return the milky liquid to the pot.

3. Stir in the honey and almond butter and mix well.

4. Thicken with the arrowroot, stirring until the mixture turns from cloudy to clear.

OAT CREAM

½ lb (225g) whole oats, cooked (see recipe for Oat Custard, p. 101
1 pint (570ml) fruit purée, e.g. pear, apricot or apple
2 teaspoons almond butter
Rice syrup, barley malt or honey to sweeten (optional)

1. Sieve or liquidize the cooked oats.

2. Blend in the fruit purée.

3. Add the almond butter and mix well. If necessary, sweeten with rice syrup, malt or honey.

FRUIT SAUCE

This makes a pleasant creamy sauce which can be made richer by the addition, after thickening, of double cream and/or brandy, for party use or for serving with Christmas puddings.

5 fl oz (140ml) unsweetened white grape juice or apple juice
5 fl oz (140ml) water
1 teaspoon almond butter
2 teaspoons arrowroot or kuzu
1 fl oz (25ml) double cream (optional)
2 fl oz (55ml) brandy (optional)

1. Add the grape juice to the water in a pot and bring to simmering point.

2. Stir in the almond butter and mix well.

3. Thicken with the arrowroot, dissolved in a little water.

4. Remove from heat and stir in the cream and brandy if using.

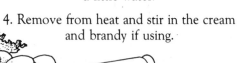

Wholesome Home Baking

Use freshly stoneground, wholegrain, organically/biodynamically grown flours for the best results. Avoid 'enriched' white flours and wheat, and use instead mixtures of whole rye, barley, maize, oat, buckwheat and millet flours. If using wheat, buy from a reliable source 100 per cent wholewheat flour or grain which has been grown without artificial fertilizers, herbicide or pesticide sprays, and which is free from dressings used after harvesting, such as preservatives and mould inhibitors.

Wheat flour, white or wholemeal, contains a higher amount of gluten than other flours. It is the gluten which gives wheat its elasticity (sponginess) and its binding properties. Therefore, in breadmaking when using alternatives to wheat, use more yeast; in baking use more raising agent, and for binding and thickening, use oatflakes, oatflour or maizemeal (unprocessed cornflour). You can adapt your own white flour recipes for wholegrain rye and barley flours, but remember, if doing so, to use a little more raising agent than is stated in the original recipe.

Sift the flour at least three times to incorporate more air (do not forget to add back the bran). 1 cup of white flour is equal in weight to ¾ cup of wholegrain flour.

Wholegrain recipes require more liquid (approximately ¼ more) and slightly less oil.

In place of white sugar, use concentrated apple juice, barley malt, brown rice syrup, real maple syrup, real honey, molasses, Barbados or Muscovado sugar. Use only ½-⅔ of the quantity suggested in the original recipe.

Commercial baking powders often contain wheat, but you can easily make your own 'Wheat-free Baking Powder'. For immediate use, for every 1 lb (455g) grain flour mix: 4 level teaspoons cream of tartar with 2 level teaspoons bicarbonate of soda. For ½ lb (225g) flour use half of these amounts.

For keeping purposes, a proportion of finely ground rice or arrowroot may be added, to prevent the ingredients caking together, e.g. 4 oz (110g) cream of tartar, 2 oz (55g) bicarbonate of soda, 4 oz (110g) ground rice or arrowroot. Sieve several times to mix, store in an airtight container and use in the amounts suggested in the following recipes.

Although the recipes do not always suggest it, it is a good idea when baking, to pre-heat the oven.

Experiment with different flours or mixtures of flours to suit your own purposes and taste. Different types and batches of wholegrain flours may require varying amounts of liquid to bind the mixture.

RYE BREAD

**2 level teaspoons unrefined sugar
¼ pint (140ml) water warmed to blood-heat
4 teaspoons dried yeast
1 lb (455g) wholemeal rye flour
1 lb (455g) wholemeal barley flour
1 tablespoon Barbados or Muscovado sugar or barley malt (optional)
1 level dessertspoon sea salt**

1. Preheat oven to 100°F/37°C.

2. Dissolve the unrefined sugar in the warm water and stir in the dried yeast. (Fresh yeast can be used if available.) Leave to froth.

3. Meanwhile put about ½ lb (225g) of wholemeal rye/barley flour into a bowl, add the Muscovado sugar and the sea salt and mix thoroughly, and then add another 1½ lb (680g) of flour.

4. Stir in the yeast mixture, adding more warm water as required, to make a stiff dough. The dough should not be sloppy, but all the flour should be wetted.

5. Divide into two bowls to allow space to rise, and place in the oven for one hour.

6. After this time, take the dough out and knead with enough flour to make a stiff, but not too dry, mixture.

7. Divide into loaves and place in previously oiled loaf tins. Score tops to make a pretty design if desired.

8. Place in oven at 100°F/37°C for a further hour to rise again. At the end of the hour turn heat up to 425°F/220°C/gas mark 7 and bake for 35 to 40 minutes.

9. Remove from oven and cool on wire rack.

Note: These quantities are sufficient for two reasonably sized loaves. Quantities can be adjusted to individual requirements. Initial attempts at this recipe tend to produce small, heavy loaves. It is well worthwhile persevering, as breadmaking is a knack which can just suddenly come. With a more compact loaf, a little goes a long way.

SPROUTED GRAIN BREAD

**1¾ lb (800g) whole oats, barley or rye kernels, organically-grown if possible
Fresh water for sprouting
Pinch of sea salt**

1. Wash the grain and soak overnight in a glass bowl or jar. (Large sweet shop jars are ideal.)

2. In the morning, strain off the soaking water and keep to use as soup stock. Rinse and drain the grains morning and evening for 2-3 days until the wholegrains have developed 1 inch (2.5cm) sprouts. Sprouting will occur more quickly in the dark. The temperature should not be too warm, but too cool a temperature will inhibit sprouting.

3. Once sprouted, grind the grains to a very fine texture using a meat grinder or a hand flour mill. A blender or liquidizer will not grind sufficiently well for the purpose.

4. Mix in the salt and place in an oiled, shallow casserole dish.

5. Cover with a lid and bake at 250°F/130°C/gas mark ½ for 4 hours, until it can be detached from the side of the pan. Remove the lid for the last 20 minutes of baking.

Variations: Minced onion, ground seeds or nuts, herbs, or soaked dried fruit can be added if liked.

SOURDOUGH RYE BREAD

**Sourdough starter (see below) plus 1½ pints (850ml) lukewarm water
1 tablespoon salt
½ lb (225g) whole or cracked rye grains
1½ lb (670g) rye flour
½ lb (225g) barley flour**

1. Mix the sourdough starter, lukewarm water and salt in a large bowl, then add the whole or cracked grain. If using whole grain, allow it to soak overnight to soften.

2. Stir in ⅓ of the mixed rye and barley flours.

3. Cover and allow to prove for 24 hours in a warm, draught-free place. An airing cupboard is ideal.

4. After 24 hours, keep back 1 lb (455g) of the mixture as the starter for the next batch of bread. This will keep for about 4 weeks in the refrigerator.

5. To the rest of the mixture add ½ pint (280ml) lukewarm water and the remainder of the rye and barley flours.

6. Put into the baking tin and prove for 4-6 hours, covered with a damp cloth. (This prevents a hard skin from forming, which makes it difficult for the loaf to rise.) Before baking, brush with water and prick with a fork, or score. Bake at 400°F/200°C/gas mark 6 for 1½ hours.

SOURDOUGH STARTER

**½ lb (225g) rye flour
½ pint (280ml) water, preferably spring water**

1. Mix the flour and water and stir until smooth.

2. Pour into a jar and leave in a warm place for about 4 days, until it smells sweet and sour.

3. Skim off any brown liquid, stir, and store in the refrigerator until required.

STEAMED RYE BREAD

Steamed flour products are more digestible than baked flour products and this method of cooking bread is well worth doing. We bought steamed rye bread in Iceland and found it to be most delicious.

For steamed bread, use the recipes given for Rye Bread (p. 104) or Sourdough Rye Bread (p. 105), but instead of putting the mixture into loaf tins for the second rising, place it in heavy ceramic or Pyrex bowls. Then follow the instructions below:

1. Allow to prove as before.

2. Cover the containers with greaseproof paper and a clean cotton cloth and tie in position securely.

3. Steam for 2-3 hours in a large pot, or 1 hour in a pressure cooker.

Variation: Herb Bread

Try adding 1 teaspoon dried herbs, e.g. caraway seeds, mixed herbs or chives to any of the bread recipes after the first proving for a tasty herb loaf, or simply use dried herbs or sesame seeds as a garnish, sprinkled over the top of proved loaves prior to baking.

VEGETABLE NUT BREAD

¾ lb (340g) mixed whole barley and rye flours
4 oz (110g) maize meal (genuine cornflour)
2 oz (55g) hazelnuts, freshly ground
2 oz (55g) chopped raisins (optional)
½ teaspoon sea salt
1 egg yolk
8 fl oz (225ml) water approximately (reduce the amount of water if vegetables are added)

Additions:
2 medium carrots, roughly grated and lightly sautéed in 1 teaspoon oil
2 medium onions, finely sliced and sautéed in 1 teaspoon oil with pinch of sea salt

1. Preheat the oven to 350°F/180°C/gas mark 4.

2. Mix the ingredients of the basic recipe, except the water, and knead well until the dough is smooth, adding a little of the water if required.

3. Add the vegetables, if using, and knead again.

4. Shape into two small loaves and place in greased pans or on a baking sheet. Bake for one hour.

INDIAN FLAT BREAD

½ lb (225g) rye or barley wholegrain flour (or mixed rye and barley flour)
½ teaspoon sea salt
2 tablespoons roasted sesame seeds
Water to mix

1. Combine the dry ingredients and add enough water to make a pliable dough.

2. Knead well until the dough is smooth and elastic.

3. Divide the mixture into 8 small pieces, form each into a ball and roll out on a floured board until a very thin pancake is formed.

4. Heat a griddle or frying pan until very hot. Cook the chapatti/pancake for ½ minute on each side until blistered and golden.

5. Set aside on a warmed plate and cover with a cloth.

6. Fold or roll and serve with lightly sautéed vegetables and a pulse sauce.

PANCAKE BATTER

These pancakes can be served with a variety of sweet or savoury fillings, and can be re-heated.

4 oz (110g) barley, rye or organic wholewheat flour
¼ teaspoon sea salt
2 eggs
2 tablespoons oil
7 fl oz (195ml) milk, soya milk or soaked raisin water
Oil for frying

1. Mix the flour with the salt and make a well in the centre.

2. Add the eggs and mix well, then the oil and finally the milk.

3. Beat well to a smooth consistency and leave to stand for about ½ hour in a cool place. Lightly re-beat before using.

4. Heat a small frying pan over a moderate heat and brush with oil.

5. Pour in 2 tablespoons of batter, enough to coat the bottom of the pan thinly. Cook for 1-2 minutes until bubbles burst on the surface and the base is cooked to a golden colour. Flip the pancake over and cook the other side.

6. Tip out on to a plate.

7. Brush the pan with oil between each pancake.

SCOTCH RYE PANCAKES

4 oz (110g) rye flour
Pinch of salt
1 level teaspoon Muscovado sugar
2 eggs
½ pint (280ml) milk
Little oil for frying

1. Mix the flour in a bowl with the salt and sugar.

2. Separate the eggs.

3. Add the yolks to the flour and beat in the milk to form a batter.

4. Whisk the whites until they peak, and fold gently into the batter.

5. Brush the pan with oil and pour off any excess.

6. Drop the batter, in tablespoon amounts, a few at a time, into the pan, and cook for 2 minutes on each side until golden brown. Keep the pancakes warm by wrapping in a clean cloth, until all the batter is used.

7. Serve warm with butter, unsweetened fruit jam or maple syrup.

SHORTCRUST PASTRY

Use this recipe for savoury or sweet pies such as lentil pie, vegetable pie, quiche, apple pie, mince pies, jam tarts etc. Use low sugar jams for jam tarts.

½ lb (225g) barley, rye or organic
wholewheat flour
5 oz (140g) butter or dairy-free margarine
Pinch of sea salt
2-4 tablespoons ice-cold water

1. Using a knife, mix the flour with the butter and the salt, until the mixture resembles fine bread crumbs.

2. Add the ice-cold water and mix with the knife to make a dough.

3. Turn on to a lightly floured board, halve and roll out thinly.

4. Use to line two greased pie tins and bake blind at 375°F/190°C/gas mark 5 for 10-15 minutes.

Note: This pastry can also be used to make Cornish or bean pasties, and covered pies, using half the pastry for the base and half for the top. Bake at 375°F/190°C/gas mark 5 for 20-30 minutes.

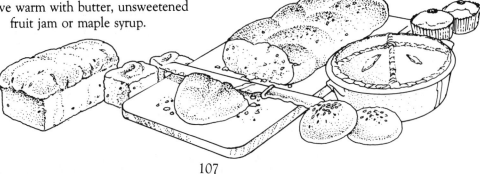

BUCKWHEAT CRÊPES

This recipe can also be made with rye or barley flour and can be used for savoury crêpes with a vegetable, bean, fish or low-fat cheese filling. It makes 12 crêpes.

6 oz (170g) buckwheat flour
¼ teaspoon sea salt
¼ teaspoon cinnamon
1 egg, well beaten
1 pint (570ml) water

1. Combine the flour, salt and cinnamon.

2. Stir in the egg and water to form a thin, smooth batter.

3. Heat a heavy skillet, brush lightly with oil, and reduce the heat to medium-low.

4. Ladle in enough batter to cover the surface of the pan, turning the pan as you add the batter, to make it spread as thinly as possible. Brown both sides.

5. To serve as a dessert, spread the crêpe with a purée of pumpkin, sweet potato, chestnut, apple butter or tahini.

OATMEAL CRUST

¾ lb (340g) rolled oats
4 oz (110g) barley, rye or organically-grown wholewheat flour
¼ teaspoon sea salt
2 tablespoons oil
½ pint (280ml) water

1. Combine the oats and the flour with the salt, add the oil and mix well.

2. Add the water and mix to a stiff dough.

3. Roll out, place in a greased pie tin and bake blind at 375°F/190°C/gas mark 5 for 10 minutes.

Note: Suggested fillings for Oatmeal Crust include: sautéed onion, carrot, cauliflower and lentil purée, chick pea sauce, bean sauce, apple pie filling, etc.

APPLE PIE FILLING

5-6 medium apples, sliced
Pinch of sea salt
2 oz (55g) rice syrup (optional) *or*
2 oz (55g) raisins
1 tablespoon water
½ teaspoon cinnamon (optional)
1 tablespoon arrowroot/kuzu

1. Stew the apples gently with the salt, syrup (or raisins) and water.

2. When soft, add the cinnamon.

3. Thicken with the arrowroot which has been dissolved in 1 tablespoon cold water.

4. Use either 6 oz (170g) of the Oatmeal Crust (p. 108) or the Barley Pastry (p. 107) to make the pie.

MINCEMEAT

1 lb (455g) cooking or eating apples
1 tablespoon water
1 tablespoon honey (optional)
1 lb (455g) mixed dried fruit (sultanas, raisins, currants)
2 oz (55g) mixed citrus peel or grated rind of 1 orange
1-2 tablespoons brandy (optional)
½ teaspoon green anise or fennel
1-2 cardamom seeds, crushed
1 teaspoon mixed spice or cinnamon

1. Core and peel the apples and stew gently in the water. If cooking apples are used, sweeten if necessary with a little honey. If eating apples are used, no sweetening should be necessary.

2. Soak the dried fruit in the brandy.

3. When the apples are soft, and while they are still warm, mix in the soaked dried fruit, the herbs and the spices.

4. Allow to stand overnight to blend the flavours, then put into jars. This will keep for 2-3 days in the refrigerator.

Note: To make Mince Pies, use the standard recipe for shortcrust pastry (p. 107).

SUPER-FAST APPLE TART

The sweetness in the raisins is sufficient to sweeten this dish without adding any sugar.

2 lb (900g) dessert apples
4 oz (110g) raisins
Pinch of sea salt
1 tablespoon water
¾ lb (340g) mixed whole grain flakes, rye, barley and oats
2 oz (55g) mixed toasted sesame and sunflower seeds
Pinch of cinnamon or mixed spice (optional)

1. Core and slice the apples and put to stew gently with the raisins, salt and water, in a covered pot.

2. Mix the whole grain flakes with the mixed seeds and put in a shallow round flan or soufflé dish.

3. Pour the apple and raisin mixture, with a pinch of cinnamon or mixed spice if desired, over the flakes and seeds. Serve hot or cold.

WHOLE OAT SCONES

4 oz (110g) whole rye, barley or organically-grown wholewheat flour
4 oz (110g) fine oatmeal
½ teaspoon bicarbonate of soda
1 teaspoon cream of tartar
½ teaspoon sea salt
2 oz (55g) butter or dairy-free margarine
¼ pint (140ml) water

1. Combine the dry ingredients.

2. Rub in the butter and add enough water to make a soft dough.

3. Knead lightly and roll out to 1 inch (2.5cm) thick. Cut into rounds, rectangles or triangles.

4. Bake at 450°F/230°C/gas mark 8 for 12 minutes.

PLAIN, SWEET OR SAVOURY SCONES

2 oz (55g) butter, dairy-free margarine or oil
½ lb (225g) rye, barley or organically-grown wholewheat flour
1 teaspoon baking powder (p. 103)
1 oz (28g) sultanas, raisins, dates or cheese (optional)
4 fl oz (110ml) water

1. Rub the butter, flour and baking powder together.

2. Add the fruit or cheese, if used.

3. Bind together with the water to make a firm dough.

4. Roll out until ¾ inch (2cm) thick, and cut into circles.

5. Bake for 10-15 minutes at 425°F/220°C/gas mark 7.

POTATO SCONES

½ lb (225g) potatoes, mashed
2 oz (55g) barley flour
1 teaspoon sea salt
Milk or water to bind, if necessary

1. Mix the potato, flour and salt together and knead well.

2. Mix to a stiff dough, adding a little milk if required.

3. Roll out on a floured board and cut into rounds.

4. Bake at 450°F/230°C/gas mark 8 for 10-12 minutes.

Variation: Add 2 oz (55g) cottage cheese or grated white Cheddar cheese to the above recipe for tasty savoury scones.

HOT CROSS BUNS

3 teaspoons unrefined sugar
2 tablespoons water, warmed
4 heaped teaspoons dried yeast
1 oz (28g) butter or oil
½ lb (225g) well-sifted wholemeal rye flour
½ lb (225g) barley flour
1 teaspoon sea salt
1 oz (28g) Muscovado sugar
4 heaped teaspoons mixed spice
2 heaped teaspoons cinnamon
2 eggs
Little apple juice
3 oz (85g) sultanas
2 oz (55g) mixed peel

1. Dissolve the unrefined sugar in the water warmed to blood-heat and add the dried yeast. Leave to froth.

2. Rub the butter into the flours and add the salt, Muscovado sugar and spice.

3. Make a well in the centre of the flour and add the yeast, mixing in well. Then add the eggs, and sufficient warmed apple juice to make a fairly stiff dough.

4. Mix in the sultanas and the peel, and allow to rise in the oven for one hour at 100°F/37°C or in any warm, draught-free place.

5. Knead slightly, and shape into about 14-18 hot cross buns.

6. Put on to a greased baking tray and mark a cross on top of each with a knife.

7. Allow to rise for a further 20 minutes at 100°F/37°C, then turn the oven up to 400°F/200°C/gas mark 6 and bake for 10-15 minutes.

VEGETABLE NUT MUFFINS

½ lb (225g) barley, rye or organically-grown wholewheat flour
1 tablespoon wheat-free baking powder (p. 103)
4 oz (110g) coarsely grated carrot
4 oz (110g) chopped walnuts
½ tablespoon honey
Pinch of sea salt
1 egg (optional)
2 tablespoons oil
8 fl oz (225ml) water

1. Sift the flour and baking powder into a bowl.

2. Stir in the carrot, walnuts, honey and salt, then gradually add the beaten egg (if using), oil and water to make a stiff batter.

3. Divide the batter between 12-24 muffin or bun tins and bake at 425°F/220°C/gas mark 7, for 20-25 minutes, until lightly browned. They should be crispy outside and soft inside.

BUCKWHEAT MUFFINS

½ lb (225g) buckwheat flour
1 tablespoon cinnamon
1 teaspoon sea salt
1 tablespoon wheat-free baking powder
(p. 103)
1 pint (570ml) water
1 tablespoon roasted sesame seeds

1. Mix all the dry ingredients except the sesame seeds.

2. Add the water gradually, mixing thoroughly to make a smooth batter.

3. Ladle the mixture into oiled muffin tins, half filling them. Sprinkle sesame seeds on top.

4. Bake for 30-40 minutes at 400°F/200°C/ gas mark 6.

ROCK CAKES

½ lb (225g) barley or organically-grown wholewheat flour
2 level teaspoons baking powder (p. 103)
4 oz (110g) Muscovado sugar
4 oz (110g) butter or dairy-free margarine
2 oz (55g) currants
1 oz (28g) mixed peel
Pinch of sea salt
1 egg
1-2 tablespoons water

1. Mix the flour, baking powder and sugar and rub in the butter.

2. Add the other dry ingredients, then the egg and enough water to make a stiff dough.

3. Put into rough heaps with a fork on a floured baking tray.

4. Bake at 425°F/220°C/gas mark 7 for 10-15 minutes.

FATLESS SPONGE

6 oz (170g) barley or organically-grown wholewheat flour
2 teaspoons baking powder (p. 103)
3 eggs
6 oz (170g) Muscovado sugar
3 tablespoons hot water

1. Sift the flour with the baking powder several times.

2. Beat the eggs and sugar until fluffy, add the flour and finally the hot water.

3. Divide the mixture between two lightly oiled sponge tins or flan tins and bake for 15-20 minutes at 350°F/180°C/gas mark 4.

SPONGE CAKES

Suitable for puddings (baked or steamed), buns, cakes, etc.

2 oz (55g) butter and 2 oz (55g) oil *or*
4 oz (110g) dairy-free margarine
3 oz (85g) Muscovado or Barbados sugar
4 oz (110g) barley or organically-grown wholemeal flour
1 teaspoon baking powder (p. 103)
2 eggs
4 tablespoons water if required

1. Cream the butter, oil and sugar.

2. Sift the flour and baking powder and add the flour and eggs alternately.

3. Finally, add the water. (Some dates, sultanas or currants may also be added if wished.)

4. Put into small cake tins or a bowl for steaming. Bake small cakes for 15-20 minutes at 350°F/180°C/gas mark 4, or steam for 2 hours.

APRICOT SPONGE FLAN

3 eggs
4 oz (110g) soft brown sugar
½ teaspoon cinnamon
2 oz (55g) arrowroot
1 oz (28g) ground almonds
4 oz (110g) dried apricots, soaked,
cooked and puréed
¼ pint (140ml) whipped cream (optional)

1. Separate the egg yolks from the whites.

2. Place the yolks and sugar in a bowl standing in a saucepan of simmering water and whisk until thick and pale.

3. Remove from the heat and continue whisking until the mixture cools.

4. With a metal spoon, gently fold in the cinnamon, arrowroot and almonds.

5. Place the egg whites in a clean, dry bowl, and whisk until stiff, then fold into the egg yolks and sugar mixture.

6. Grease an 8 inch (20cm) sandwich tin and line with greaseproof paper.

7. Turn the mixture into the tin, and bake at 350°F/180°C/gas mark 4, for 25-30 minutes, or until the cake springs back when lightly pressed.

8. Turn on to a wire rack to cool and remove the greaseproof paper.

9. Cut the cake in half and spread with the apricot purée and half the whipped cream.

10. Sandwich together and decorate with the remaining whipped cream.

BLACK FOREST GÂTEAU

For very special occasions only.
Instead of black cherries you can also use peaches or plums mixed with whipped cream.

4 oz (110g) butter or dairy-free margarine
3 oz (85g) Muscovado sugar
4 oz (110g) wholemeal rye flour lightly sifted
4 oz (110g) wholemeal barley flour
2 rounded dessertspoons carob powder
1 teaspoon baking powder (p. 103)
2 eggs
2-4 tablespoons water or apple juice
¼ pint (140ml) whipped cream (optional)
4 oz (110g) black cherries
4 oz (110g) carob chocolate or chocolate flake (optional)

1. Cream the butter and sugar.

2. Mix together the flours, carob powder and baking powder, and add alternately with the eggs.

3. Finally add the water or apple juice.

4. Divide between two small flan tins and bake at 350°F/180°C/gas mark 4 for about 30 minutes.

5. Turn on to a wire rack and allow to cool.

6. Slit each cake in half and sandwich the 4 layers together with a mixture of black cherries and whipped cream.

7. Cover the top and sides of the cake with more whipped cream and decorate with crumbled carob chocolate or chocolate flake (optional) and whole cherries.

CAROB CAKE

4 oz (110g) butter, dairy-free margarine
or oil
2 tablespoons honey, barley malt or
maple syrup
2 oz (55g) Muscovado or Barbados sugar
2 eggs
1 oz (28g) carob powder
3½ oz (100g) barley or organically
grown wholemeal flour
1 teaspoon wheat-free baking powder
(p. 103)
2 oz (55g) sunflower seeds, hazelnuts or
walnuts
2 oz (55g) sultanas
Cold water or milk to mix

1. Pre-heat the oven to 350°F/180°C/gas
mark 4.

2. Lightly grease an 8 inch (20cm) cake tin
and dust with flour.

3. Cream the butter, honey and sugar, then
beat in the eggs.

4. Sieve in the carob powder, flour and
baking powder, adding back the bran in the
sieve.

5. Add the nuts and sultanas with sufficient
water or milk to give a dropping consistency.

6. Transfer the mixture to the tin and bake
in the centre of the oven for 20-25 minutes.
Allow to cool slightly before turning out.

ICE BOX CAKE

10 oz (280g) muesli
2 tablespoons oil
2 tablespoons honey
2 oz (55g) cashew nuts, finely ground
3 tablespoons tahini
6 fl oz (170ml) hot water
1 lb (455g) eating apples
1 lemon, freshly squeezed

1. Mix the muesli with the oil and honey,
and dry-roast in a frying pan until golden.

2. Combine the muesli mix with the cashew
nuts, tahini and hot water.

3. Grate the apples and coat in lemon juice.

4. Oil an 8 inch (20cm) cake tin. Press in
half the mixture, spread with grated apple
and then top with the remaining mixture.

5. Press down well to smooth the surface.
Cover and place in the refrigerator for 12
hours.

6. Turn out, slice and serve.

WALNUT CAKE

4½ oz (125g) shelled walnuts
4 eggs
4 oz (110g) Muscovado sugar
Tiny pinch of nutmeg (optional)
Pinch of mixed spice (optional)

1. Grind the walnuts finely.

2. Separate the egg yolks from the whites
and beat the yolks with the sugar for 10-15
minutes until thick.

3. Stir in the ground walnuts and the spices.

4. Beat the egg whites stiffly and fold gently
into the mixture.

5. Divide the mixture between 2 lightly
greased sandwich tins, lined with greaseproof
paper and bake at 350°F/180°C/gas mark 4
for 25-30 minutes.

6. Sandwich together with muscovado sugar
butter icing and chopped walnuts or a nut
spread.

GINGER SPICE LOAF

4 oz (110g) whole rye flour and 4 oz (110g) whole barley flour *or* ½ lb (225g) organically-grown wholewheat flour
1 teaspoon baking powder (p. 103)
¼ teaspoon mixed spice
¼ teaspoon ginger
¼ teaspoon green anise (optional)
1-2 cardamom seeds, crushed (optional)
4 fl oz (110ml) oil
2 oz (55g) Muscovado sugar
1 tablespoon crude black molasses
6 oz (170g) dried fruit, sultanas, raisins, etc.
1 egg

1. Mix the flour, baking powder and spices.

2. Warm the oil, sugar and molasses together and stir into the dry ingredients.

3. Add the dried fruit and finally the beaten egg.

4. Mix to a fairly stiff consistency. If necessary, add a little milk.

5. Turn into a greased loaf tin and bake for 1¼ hours at 350°F/180°C/gas mark 4.

BOILED FRUIT CAKE

2 oz (55g) butter and 2 fl oz (55ml) oil *or* 4 oz (110g) dairy-free margarine
4 oz (110g) Muscovado or Barbados sugar
6 oz (170g) currants
6 oz (170g) sultanas
2 oz (55g) candied peel
1 oz (28g) glacé cherries
8 fl oz (225ml) water or unsweetened apple juice
1 level teaspoon baking soda
1 level teaspoon mixed spice
2 beaten eggs
4 oz (110g) whole rye flour and 4 oz (110g) whole barley flour *or* ½ lb (225g) organically-grown wholewheat flour

1. Place all the ingredients except the eggs and flour in a pan and boil for one minute. Allow to cool.

2. Line an 8 inch (20cm) cake tin with greaseproof paper.

3. Add the eggs and the flour to the cooled mixture and beat well.

4. Bake in a moderate oven, 375°F/190°C/gas mark 5, for 1¼ hours.

FARMHOUSE FRUIT CAKE

3 oz (85g) butter and 3 fl oz (85ml) oil *or* 6 oz (170g) dairy-free margarine
4 oz (110g) Barbados or Muscovado sugar
2 large eggs
4 oz (110g) wholemeal rye flour lightly sifted and 4 oz (110g) wholemeal barley flour *or* ½ lb (225g) organically-grown wholewheat flour
1 teaspoon baking powder (p. 103)
10 oz (280g) mixed dried fruit
2 oz (55g) glacé cherries
1 teaspoon mixed spice

1. Cream the butter, oil and sugar until light and fluffy.

2. Add the eggs and flour (with the baking powder) alternately and then mix in the dried fruit, the glacé cherries and the spice.

3. Place in a greased and lined 8 inch (20cm) round, deep cake tin. Smooth the top.

4. Bake in the middle of a pre-heated oven at 325°F/170°C/gas mark 3 for 1½-2 hours.

BAKED FRUIT SALAD CAKE

1 teaspoon each of baking soda and
cream of tartar
4 oz (110g) wholegrain flour (barley, rye
or organically-grown wholewheat)
6 oz (170g) chopped dates
3 oz (85g) currants
4 fl oz (110ml) apple juice
Rind and juice of one lemon
¾ lb (340g) rolled oats
½ teaspoon sea salt
1 teaspoon cinnamon
2 oz (55g) roasted, flaked nuts or
sunflower seeds
1 oz (28g) sesame seeds
1-2 eggs

1. Heat the oven to 350°F/180°C/gas
mark 4.

2. Add the raising agent to the flour.

3. Cook the fruit in the juices for 5 minutes,
then add to the flour and remaining dry
ingredients.

4. Beat the eggs and add.

5. Mix well to a soft texture and bake in a
greased, lined tin for 40 minutes.

6. Cool and cut into squares.

HIGHLAND OATCAKES

2 tablespoons oil
3-4 tablespoons boiling water to mix
½ lb (225g) fine oatmeal
½ teaspoon sea salt
½ teaspoon sodium bicarbonate

1. Warm the oil and mix with the boiling
water.

2. Pour into the dry ingredients and mix to a
stiff paste.

3. Turn on to a board dusted with oatmeal.
Quickly roll into a round about ⅛ inch
(½cm) thick.

4. Cut into quarters and cook slowly on a
griddle until hardened.

5. Put into a cool oven for about ½ hour to
dry.

6. Alternatively, the oatcakes can be baked
at 350°F/180°C/gas mark 4 for 20-25
minutes.

LOUISE'S OATCAKES

1 oz (28g) sesame seeds
5 oz (140g) pinhead oatmeal or whole
oats
2 oz (55g) dry toasted pot barley grains
Pinch of bicarbonate of soda
1 level teaspoon of sea salt
2 tablespoons oil (sesame is particularly
good)
4 fl oz (110ml) hot water, just off the boil

1. Combine the seeds, oats and barley and
grind finely in a coffee mill or hand mill.
These can be pre-roasted to add extra
flavour.

2. Add the bicarbonate of soda and the salt
and mix well.

3. Then using a wooden spoon add in the
oil, mixing to a 'breadcrumb' texture.

4. Add the hot water, mixing to a stiff dough
with the wooden spoon or a knife. Knead
lightly in the bowl.

5. Divide in half and roll out to ⅛ inch
(½cm) thickness on a board which has been
lightly dusted with rye or barley flour. Half
way through rolling, the dough can be
sprinkled with extra sesame seeds.

6. Divide the dough into triangles, rectangles
or circles and bake on a greased biscuit tray
for 15-20 minutes at 375°F/190°C/gas
mark 5.

7. Cool and then store in an air-tight tin.

SHEILA'S CHRISTMAS CAKE

2 lb (900g) mixed dried fruit (sultanas, raisins, currants)
¾ lb (340g) mixed citrus peel
3 fl oz (85ml) brandy
1 lb (455g) wholegrain flakes (rye, oats, barley)
6 oz (170ml) unsweetened, additive-free grape or apple juice
½ lb (225g) butter or dairy-free margarine
½ lb (225g) Barbados or Muscovado sugar
6 fl oz (170ml) oil
½ oz (14g) baking powder (p. 103)
1 teaspoon mixed spice
1 lb (455g) barley, rye or organically-grown wholewheat flour
4 eggs

1. Soak the fruit and peel in the brandy and allow to stand overnight in a covered dish.

2. Soak the flakes in the grape or apple juice.

3. Cream the butter and sugar and then add the oil gradually, beating again until well creamed.

4. Mix the baking powder and the mixed spice with the flour and sift three times, being careful to add back all the bran.

5. Add the eggs and the flour alternately to the creamed butter and sugar, and then beat in the soaked flakes.

6. Finally stir in the fruit and any brandy that has not been absorbed. Moisten to the usual cake consistency with a little grape or apple juice if necessary.

7. Line a large round or square cake tin with greaseproof paper and grease well.

8. Turn the mixture into the tin and bake in an oven pre-heated to 350°F/180°C/gas mark 4, for 2-2½ hours until the cake is ready.

9. Cover with marzipan and decorate as desired.

Note: This cake tastes good but does tend to crumble on cutting.

CHRISTMAS CAKE

This mixture makes a 7½ lb (3.5kg) cake.

½ lb (225g) butter and 8 fl oz (225ml) oil
or 1 lb (455g) dairy-free margarine
1 lb (455g) Barbados or Muscovado sugar
8 eggs (free-range if possible)
2 lb (900g) organically-grown wholewheat flour *or* 1 lb (455g) rye flour and 1 lb (455g) barley flour
½ oz (14g) baking powder (p. 103)
1 lb (455g) sultanas
1 lb (455g) currants
¾ lb (340g) mixed peel
Apple juice to mix

1. Cream the butter, oil and sugar.

2. Add the eggs one at a time, adding a little flour after each one to prevent the mixture from curdling.

3. When all the eggs have been added, mix in the remainder of the flour with the baking powder, and then the fruit, moistening to the usual cake consistency with a little apple juice.

4. Bake in a large round or square well-papered and greased tin, at 350°F/180°C/gas mark 4, for 2 to 2½ hours.

5. Turn on to wire rack and allow to cool.

6. Cover with marzipan and decorate as desired.

LOBELIA CAKE

This recipe can be used as a cake or a fruit loaf.

½ lb (225g) barley or organically grown
wholewheat flour
1 oz (28g) ground almonds
1 teaspoon baking powder (p. 103)
2 oz (55g) butter and 2 oz (55ml) oil *or*
4 oz (110g) dairy-free margarine
3 oz (85g) Muscovado sugar
2 eggs
Little apple juice
1 oz (28g) pine kernels (optional)
3 oz (85g) sunflower seeds
2 oz (55g) sesame seeds
2 oz (55g) raisins

1. Mix the flour, ground almonds and baking powder.

2. In a separate bowl, cream the butter, oil and sugar.

3. Beat in one egg and then some of the flour mixture. Continue adding egg and flour alternately, and mix to a soft texture using the apple juice.

4. Then mix in the pine kernels, sunflower seeds, sesame seeds and raisins.

5. Put into a lightly oiled, medium-sized loaf tin and bake at 325°F/170°C/gas mark 3 for 30-40 minutes.

OAT BISCUITS

3 oz (85g) barley malt
12 fl oz (340ml) water
2 tablespoons oil
¾ lb (340g) oat or barley flakes
½ teaspoon salt
2 oz (55g) whole rye, barley or
organically-grown wheatflour
2 oz (55g) roasted sunflower seeds
½ teaspoon almond essence

1. Heat the malt, water and oil together in a pot. This allows slightly less flour and more flakes to be used. Making the mixture slightly wet is easier on the digestion.

2. Mix the oatflakes, salt and flour and stir into the heated ingredients. Mix well to a soft dropping consistency.

3. Add the dry roasted sunflower seeds and the almond essence.

4. Drop in tablespoon quantities on to a lightly oiled baking tray and flatten slightly or spread the mixture in the baking tray and cut into squares when baked.

5. Bake for 30 minutes at 375°F/190°C/gas mark 5.

OATMEAL RAISIN COOKIES

2 oz (55g) raisins
1 teaspoon sea salt
12 fl oz (340ml) water
1 oz (28g) barley malt or maple syrup
½ teaspoon vanilla essence
¾ lb (340g) rolled oats
4 oz (110g) whole rye, barley or
organically-grown wheatflour
2 tablespoons oil

1. Put the raisins and salt into a pot with the water and cook for 5 minutes.

2. Remove from the heat, stir in the syrup and the vanilla essence and allow to cool.

3. Mix the oats, the flour and the oil together in a bowl, rubbing well with the fingers.

4. Pour the liquid into the dry ingredients and stir to mix.

5. Drop the mixture in spoonfuls on to an oiled baking sheet, flatten each slightly and bake at 375°F/190°C/gas mark 5, until golden brown, about 20 minutes.

CAPE COD OATMEAL COOKIES

1 egg
1 oz (28g) honey
3-4 tablespoons oil
1 tablespoon treacle
1 teaspoon baking soda
1 teaspoon cinnamon
1 lb (455g) rolled oats
2 oz (55g) raisins or walnuts
½ lb (225g) barley flour
Little apple juice or water to moisten, if required

1. Beat the egg lightly.

2. Add the other ingredients and mix well.

3. Drop by spoonfuls on to a buttered baking tray, and press flat with the fingers or a fork.

4. Bake at 325°F/170°C/gas mark 3, for 15 minutes.

ARROWROOT CREAM BISCUITS

6 oz (170g) butter or dairy-free margarine
2 oz (55g) raw cane sugar, powdered in a grinder
6 oz (170g) wholemeal barley or organically-grown wheat flour
2 oz (55g) arrowroot

1. Cream the butter and sugar, and add the dry ingredients.

2. Roll into walnut-sized balls.

3. Put on to a greased baking tray and flatten with a fork.

4. Bake at 350°F/180°C/gas mark 4 for 15 minutes.

5. Use plain or sandwiched together with butter icing.

NUTTY BISCUITS

2 oz (55g) butter and 2 fl oz (55ml) oil *or*
4 oz (110g) dairy-free margarine
1 tablespoon barley malt
2 oz (55g) Muscovado sugar
4 oz (110g) rye, barley or organically grown wholewheat flour
½ lb (225g) porridge oats or barley flakes
1 tablespoon flaked hazelnuts or almonds

1. Melt the butter, oil, malt and sugar and pour over all the dry ingredients except the nuts.

2. Mix well.

3. Form into balls and place on a baking sheet.

4. Flatten with a fork, sprinkle with the flaked nuts and bake for 15 minutes at 350°F/180°C/gas mark 4.

WALNUT BISCUITS

¾ lb (340g) rolled oats
¾ lb (340g) barley, rye or organically-grown wholewheat flour
1 teaspoon sea salt
4 fl oz (110ml) oil
4 oz (110g) maple or brown rice syrup, or barley malt
6 oz (170g) toasted walnut pieces
1 tablespoon vanilla essence
6 fl oz (170ml) water

1. Preheat the oven to 350°F/180°C/gas mark 4.

2. Mix the oats, the flour and the salt, then stir in the oil and the syrup or malt, the walnuts, the essence and the water to form a spreadable mixture.

3. Drop on to a lightly oiled biscuit tray in teaspoon or dessertspoon amounts and flatten slightly.

4. Bake for 18-20 minutes.

DREAMY TRUFFLES

Another Christmas treat.

**5 oz (140g) plain chocolate or carob
chocolate
½ oz (15g) carrageen or agar-agar
4 fl oz (110ml) unsweetened apple juice
2 tablespoons kirsch or rum (optional)
4 oz (110g) chestnut purée
Chocolate vermicelli or powdered raw
cane sugar to coat (optional)**

1. Melt the chocolate in a bowl over a pot of boiling water.

2. While the chocolate is melting, simmer the carrageen or agar-agar in the apple juice until the flakes are soft and gelatinous.

3. Cool a little and stir in the kirsch or rum if used.

4. Beat the puréed chestnut into the melted chocolate until smooth and well mixed, and then beat in the carrageen or agar-agar mix.

5. Allow to cool and to stiffen sufficiently to roll into balls.

6. Roll in the chocolate vermicelli and put in the fridge to harden.

7. Alternatively, divide the mixture into two and pile on to silver foil or non-stick baking paper in log shapes.

8. Roll in the foil and put in the refrigerator overnight.

9. Just before serving, unroll, slice into rounds and dust the surfaces with icing sugar.

FLAPJACKS

This recipe makes 8 flapjacks.

**5 oz (140g) butter, dairy-free margarine
or oil
2 tablespoons honey, barley malt or
maple syrup
1 oz (28g) Barbados or Muscovado sugar
½ lb (225g) rolled oats**

1. Lightly grease an 8 inch (20cm) square, shallow cake tin.

2. Gently heat the butter, honey and sugar in a pot until melted.

3. Stir in the oats, remove from the heat and turn the mixture into the tin.

4. Smooth the mixture and bake in a pre-heated oven at 350°F/180°C/gas mark 4 for 20 minutes. Allow to cool before removing from the tin.

Variations:
1. Reduce the oats to 4 oz (110g) and add 4 oz (110g) chopped dates, raisins or chopped apricots.

2. Use half oats and half muesli containing nuts, seeds and dried fruit.

3. Reduce the oats to 6 oz (170g) and add 2 oz (55g) sunflower seeds or 1 oz (28g) desiccated coconut and 1 oz (28g) sesame seeds.

4. Reduce the oats to 7 oz (200g) and add 1 oz (28g) flaked or chopped almonds and the grated rind of a lemon.

5. Use 2 tablespoons molasses treacle and the rind of a lemon in place of the 2 tablespoons honey.

6. Use 2 tablespoons apple purée in place of the 2 tablespoons honey.

SUNFLOWER SEED BISCUITS

**6 oz (170g) freshly ground sunflower seeds
4 oz (110g) barley, brown rice or organically-grown wholewheat flour
1 tablespoon barley malt, brown rice syrup or honey
2 tablespoons oil
½ crisp apple, grated
Pinch of sea salt
1 egg, beaten, or 2 tablespoons ice-cold water, to bind**

1. Mix all the ingredients well.

2. If egg is used, drop the mixture in teaspoonful amounts on to a greased baking sheet.

3. If water is used, knead the mixture, roll into balls and flatten on the baking tray.

4. Bake for 30 minutes at 350°F/180°C/gas mark 4, then remove from the baking sheet or tray and allow to cool on a wire rack.

PARKINS

**2 tablespoons oil
2 oz (55g) Muscovado sugar
1 oz (28g) crude black molasses
4 oz (110g) rye, barley or organically-grown wholewheat flour
4 oz (110g) fine oatmeal
¼ teaspoon mixed spice
¼ teaspoon cinnamon
½ teaspoon ginger
¼ teaspoon bicarbonate of soda**

1. Warm the oil, sugar and molasses together.

2. Add to the dry ingredients, mixing to form a fairly stiff dough.

3. Roll into small balls using the hands and place on a greased baking sheet.

4. Bake at 350°F/180°C/gas mark 4, for about 15 minutes, then cool on a wire rack.

BARLEY DIGESTIVES

This recipe makes 20 biscuits.

**3½ oz (100g) barley flour
1½ oz (45g) fine oatmeal
½ teaspoon wheat-free baking powder (p. 103)
Pinch of sea salt
2 oz (55g) butter, dairy-free margarine or oil
1 tablespoon Barbados or Muscovado sugar (optional)
2-3 tablespoons ice-cold water, cow's, goat's or soya milk**

1. Pre-heat the oven to 350°F/180°C/gas mark 4.

2. Lightly grease a baking tray.

3. Sieve the flour, oatmeal, baking powder and salt into the mixing bowl, adding the bran from the sieve.

4. Rub in the butter and stir in the sugar and enough water or milk to make a soft dough.

5. Knead lightly, then roll out on a lightly floured surface to ⅛ inch (0.3cm).

6. Cut out the biscuits using a 3 inch (7.5cm) round cutter.

7. Place on the tray, prick with a fork and bake in the oven for 15 minutes.

8. Transfer to a cooling rack, and then store in an airtight tin.

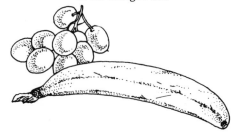

ALMOND AND APRICOT CRUNCHY BAR

4 fl oz (110ml) oil
3 oz (85g) Muscovado sugar
1 egg (free-range if possible)
4 oz (110g) wholemeal rye or barley flour
4 oz (110g) mixed rye, oat and barley flakes
4 oz (110g) chopped almonds
6 oz (170g) chopped dried apricots

1. Cream the oil and sugar. Add the egg and beat well.

2. Mix in the flour and the flakes and then add the chopped almonds and apricots.

3. Put the mixture into a flat rectangular buttered baking tin and bake at 375°F/190°C/gas mark 5 for about 30 minutes.

4. Mark into pieces while still warm and allow to cool before removing from tin.

KIRKINTILLOCH SLICES

1½ oz (45g) butter and 1½ fl oz (45ml) oil
or 3 oz (85g) dairy-free margarine
2 oz (55g) Muscovado or Barbados sugar
3 oz (85g) barley or organically-grown wholewheat flour
1 teaspoon baking powder (p. 103)
2 eggs
5 oz (140g) chopped dates
2 oz (55g) sultanas
2 oz (55g) chopped walnuts

1. Cream the butter, oil and sugar. Mix the flour and baking powder.

2. Beat one egg and half of the flour into the butter mixture, then the other egg and the rest of the flour. Mix in the chopped fruit and the walnuts.

3. Put into a greased Swiss roll tin and bake for 20 minutes at 375°F/190°C/gas mark 5. When cold, cut into slices.

ROUNDELWOOD SHORTBREAD

½ lb (225g) butter or dairy-free margarine
4 oz (110g) Muscovado sugar
½ lb (225g) barley flour
4 oz (110g) brown rice flour

1. Cream the butter and sugar and add the flours.

2. Roll out and cut into rounds.

3. Bake for 15 minutes at 350°F/180°C/gas mark 4.

A MATTER OF THIRST

Or the when, what, why and how of drinking.

Drinking a toast to someone's health is a friendly gesture, but the overconsumption of fluid, whether alcoholic, sweetened or just plain water, is a less than healthy practice.

Advice to drink according to thirst is not ideal, as an artificial thirst can easily be created by eating certain foods. The consumption of the concentrated flavour foods, such as salt, shoyu, miso, spices, sugars, honey and other sweetened and highly seasoned foods tend to increase the desire for fluids. Many fluids are themselves far from thirst-quenching. Milk, for example, is more of a food than a drink; soft drinks, lemonades and squashes, are high in sugar or artificial sweetener and other additives; fruit juices are concentrated sources of fruit sugar, without the natural fibre of the fruit pulp which normally limits one's consumption. Some children are highly sensitive to artificial colouring in orange squash, resulting in aggressiveness, irritability, or what has been termed hyperactivity.

Tea and coffee are stimulant drinks which increase the metabolic stress on the mind and body. The caffeine and tannin contents of these drinks are the main culprits. But certain good quality leaf teas are low in tannin and caffeine and Japanese twig tea is a nourishing, non-stimulant drink and a useful source of calcium. It is particularly suitable for children, nursing mothers and the elderly as well as being an enjoyable and refreshing drink. Roasted cereal/grain and dandelion root drinks make good coffee alternatives. All are pleasant to taste and do not disturb sleep.

Beers, spirits and wines are for moderate use only. It is all too easy to get into a daily drinking habit, a couple of pints of beer with lunch or after work, a whisky to relax you before dinner, a sherry in the afternoon, a glass or two of wine with your evening meal, a gin and tonic while watching TV – innocent enough but definitely detrimental to the liver (as is the regular use of vinegar and vinegar pickles).

The overconsumption of any fluid including water is harmful to the system, increasing hypertension and overworking the kidneys. But the less meat and seasoning you use, the less water you require. Those who base their eating on wholegrains and vegetables receive much of their fluid from their food. Wholegrains can absorb all the water in which they are cooked and vegetables vary in their water content, a cucumber being higher in water than a carrot.

Four cups of hot or room temperature water a day, sipped slowly, should be more than adequate for the needs of a healthy adult who is following the dietary suggestions outlined in this book.

FRUIT FIZZ

¼ pint (140ml) unsweetened fruit juice
1 slice lemon
1 pint (570ml) sparkling spring water

1. Mix the ingredients and serve at once, cool but not chilled.

BOILED BARLEY WATER

2 tablespoons barley kernels
1 pint (570ml) water
Juice of a lemon
1 tablespoon honey to taste

1. Place all the ingredients into a pot and boil gently for 30-40 minutes, until the barley softens.

2. Strain off the liquid and serve hot or cold.

BARLEY OR BROWN RICE TEA

4oz (110g) dry cereal grain (barley or short grain brown rice)
1 pint (570ml) water

1. Wash and drain the grain, then dry-roast in a medium oven or in a heavy pot over a medium heat, stirring constantly with a wooden spoon or spatula until toasted (golden brown but not burnt).

2. Cool and store in an airtight container.

3. Measure out 1 tablespoon roasted grain into the water in a heavy pot with a tight-fitting lid.

4. Bring to the boil and then simmer for 15 minutes.

5. Strain and serve hot or cold. There is no need to add milk or sweetener.

Note: For extra flavour, stir in 1 dessertspoon green leaf tea to the above and infuse for 2-3 minutes before serving, or simmer 1 tablespoon roasted twig tea along with the roasted grain for 15 minutes. Strain and serve as before.

ROASTED DANDELION ROOT COFFEE

Pieces of dandelion root can be bought ready dried and roasted and will store well in an airtight container.
It looks like percolated coffee and has a distinctive, likeable flavour, and can be drunk without milk or sweetener. It is free of caffeine and is therefore suitable for anyone with a weak digestion or heart problem. It is also a mild diuretic.

1 tablespoon dandelion root
1 pint (570ml) water

1. Simmer the dandelion root in the water. The longer the cooking (simmer for 5-15 minutes), the better the flavour. If too strong for your taste, simply dilute with hot water.

BANCHA TWIG TEA

Also known as Kukicha or 3-year tea. It is made from the winter-harvested and roasted twigs of three-year-old tea bushes.
This is an ideal, non-stimulant after-meal drink and a useful source of calcium. Left-over twigs and tea can be re-used.

2 tablespoons twig tea
1 pint (570ml) water

1. Simmer the twigs in the water for 10-20 minutes.

2. Strain, dilute to taste and serve without milk or sweetener.

UMESHOBANCHA

This drink is excellent when the appetite is poor and can also be used to relieve headaches and the symptoms of head-colds and 'flu.

⅓ pint (200ml) bancha twig tea
1 teaspoon tamari/shoyu soya sauce
½ teaspoon umeboshi paste
Pinch of powdered ginger or 1 teaspoon fresh ginger juice

1. Heat the tea and pour over the remaining ingredients in a cup or mug. Stir to mix.

2. Use hot as a reviving drink.

HERB TEAS

Herbal tea bags are available commercially, and are convenient, but for real enjoyment, use freshly picked or fresh dried whole leaves, flowers or seeds of recommended plants. Herbs can be grown easily in most gardens and many can be grown successfully indoors. There is a wide variety of specialist books on the subject which give detailed descriptions of what herbs to grow, and how to harvest and store them. Some of the best dried herbs come from Provence in France, where they are specially grown for tea-making and medicinal use.

Although dried herbs can be kept in an airtight container in a cool, dry place almost indefinitely, there will be a loss of flavour, and stocks should be replaced annually, with the coming of the new season's crops.

Herbs are best taken for their reviving, refreshing or relaxing effect, and not drunk along with meals or snacks.

Herbs should be picked only where you can be sure they are free from pesticide or herbicide sprays, and away from roadside pollution.

It is best to use carbon-filtered or bottled spring water, as traces of chlorine and metals such as aluminium, lead and copper can adversely affect the taste of herbal teas.

In the following recipes, use 1 pint (570ml) boiling water for 4 cups of tea.

ANISE AND LINDEN FLOWER TEA

Refreshing and calming.

1 teaspoon dried anise/aniseed
1 tablespoon (½ cup) dried lime/linden flowers and leaves
2 teaspoons crushed, dried mint or 4 fresh mint leaves

or

2 teaspoons cassis (dried blackcurrant leaves) (optional)

FENNEL TEA

A digestive aid.

2 teaspoons fennel seed
1 sprig fresh or dried fennel herb

ELDERFLOWER TEA

Refreshing and diuretic.

1 tablespoon dried, or 2 tablespoons fresh, elder flowers (picked before the flowers begin to fade)
Juice of ½ fresh lemon
1 teaspoon honey per cup (optional)

ANISE AND HONEY TEA

2 teaspoons dried anise/aniseed
1 teaspoon honey per cup

1. Warm a pottery, china, heatproof glass or enamel coated container (teapot or jug), by rinsing in boiling water.

2. Dry the container and add the measured herbs.

3. Pour on the boiling water, cover with the lid or a saucer, and leave to infuse ('brew') for 2-5 minutes, depending on the desired strength of the tea.

4. Strain the tea into cups, and stir in honey.

Other refreshing herb teas which can be made in a similar way include: chamomile, dandelion (diuretic), dill, ginger root (dispels wind/flatulence), lemon balm (delicious with honey), lemon verbena, maté, mint — applemint, pennyroyal, peppermint, spearmint — nettle (diuretic), raspberry leaves, rooibosch (South African) and sage.

Grain 'Coffees'

There are many varieties of grain coffee made from roasted barley, rye and chicory. They are additive-free and caffeine-free. Use like any instant coffee.

Catherine's Hot Apple Punch

This is good for serving to weary travellers on cold winter nights.

½ lb (225g) mixed sultanas and raisins
4 oz (110g) mixed peel, finely chopped
1½ fresh lemons
10 whole dried cloves
¼ pint (140ml) boiling water
6 pints (3.4 litres) pure, unsweetened, cloudy apple juice
6 oz (170g) runny honey
1½ teaspoons ground cinnamon or a 2 inch (5cm) cinnamon stick
3 fl oz (85ml) brandy

1. Overnight, soak the dried fruit and half a fresh lemon pierced with 10 cloves, in the boiling water topped up with sufficient apple juice to cover the fruit.

2. The next day, put the remaining apple juice and the soaked fruit mixture into a large enamelled or stainless steel pot.

3. Add the juice of one fresh lemon and warm the mixture slightly.

4. Stir in the honey until completely dissolved and add the ground cinnamon or cinnamon stick.

5. Heat to the desired temperature, simmered not boiled.

6. Just before serving, stir in the brandy and strain the punch into warmed jugs or a punch bowl.

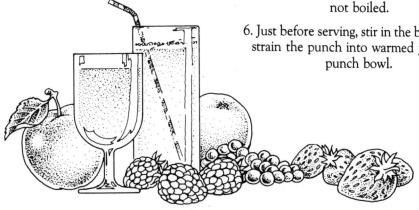

Menu Suggestions

In the beginning it does take longer to prepare wholefood meals. Planning ahead is of great importance in order, for example, that the beans are pre-soaked and grains are given time to cook. But there are pulses, such as brown lentils, that require no pre-soaking and there are grains that cook quickly, such as buckwheat and millet.

For quick meals and snacks, all you require are the appropriate basic ingredients. The recipes on pages 67-72 give a few 'instant' ideas for wholesome fast foods. In fact, most of the recipes in the main meals section can be hastily assembled using left-over or pre-cooked ingredients.

A nourishing, appetizing and satisfying way to cater for teenage hunger pangs comes in the shape of a warming bowl of broth soup, which is ideal also for lunch when teamed with beanspread on rye crispbread or toast, and served with a saucerful of seasonal salad.

The compensations for a little extra time spent in the kitchen are delicious, inexpensive meals and an increasingly healthful family and self.

Cooking can be an enjoyable therapy if it is regarded as such, rather than a chore. Working with fresh, whole, seasonal ingredients is a creative experience calling on the basics of artistry – the use of colour and texture. The rich greens of broccoli and watercress contrast vividly with the warm orangey red of carrots, the cool icy white of turnip and the cream and yellows of swede, sweetcorn and cauliflower.

Those used to the 'pure' white of refined cereals and sugar show distinct colour prejudice with regard to wholegrains. But even these are far from dull. The rich brown of roasted buckwheat, the yellow of millet (made more so when served with green and orange vegetables) and the two-tone cream and fawn of brown rice all team well with the vast range of pulses, including aduki beans, chick peas and brown and green lentils.

For varied texture, serve smooth sauces and grain dishes with lightly cooked vegetables, crunchy salads, toasted seeds and savoury crumble toppings.

The real test of a 'balanced' meal is a feeling of both taste and appetite satisfaction at its conclusion. To achieve this it has been suggested that each meal should comprise ingredients which provide the five tastes, namely sweet, sour, salt, bitter and pungent or spicy. Foods providing these tastes include the following:

Sweet. Wholegrain cereals, well chewed; ripe fruit, fresh or dried; honey; maple syrup; grain syrups; sugars; and brown rice and barley malts. Onions and vegetables such as carrots, parsnips, swedes, squash and pumpkin, especially when sautéed, also provide a sweet flavour.

Sour. Lemon; lactofermented pickles such as sauerkraut and umeboshi plums; brown rice vinegar and ume vinegar.

Salt. Sea salt; miso; tamari/shoyu soya sauce; sea vegetables; salty condiments such as tekka.

Bitter. Dandelion greens, endive, chicory and other green leafy vegetables; bitter spices such as nutmeg; bitter herbs such as wormwood, tansy, rue and sorrel; coffee; tea; charcoal; roasted or burned foods.

Pungent or *spicy.* Ginger; radish; watercress; blue cheese; pepper; curry; fresh horseradish; mustard.

Used together, each taste acts to enhance the others, for example:

A rich miso soup (salt) with a garnish of fresh lemon wedge (sour) and a sprig of watercress (pungent or spicy);

Steamed endive or chicory (bitter) with a ginger-arrowroot (spicy) aduki bean sauce (salt);

Brown rice (sweet – made more so by cooking with a pinch of sea salt) and lactofermented pickles or sauerkraut (sour);

Apple juice jelly made from unsweetened apple juice (sweet) and agar-agar (a seaweed, salt).

In most meals it will be noted that the sweet taste is mainly provided by wholegrains and balanced by smaller amounts of salt, spicy, bitter and sour foods. In this way, unnatural cravings for sugary foods are diminished.

Some people find their digestion improved by eating less complex meals comprising predominantly protein (animal foods, i.e. meats, fish, eggs, cheese) *or* predominantly starch food (wholegrains, pulses). Predominantly protein foods combine well with vegetables, especially leafy greens and salads, fresh fruits and wines. Predominantly starch foods combine well with both root and leafy vegetables, lightly cooked rather than raw, and with small amounts of nuts, seeds and fruits, either soaked dried fruit or poached, baked or stewed fresh fruit, or agar-agar fruit jellies.

Starch and sugar combinations, such as bread and jam (or marmalade) or puddings, cakes and biscuits, often lead to indigestion and an expanded stomach and intestines, resulting from fermentation of the food in the stomach.

The optional ingredients suggested in the preceding recipes are to be included as liked and tolerated. The menu ideas which follow act as a guide, demonstrating how the recipes given in this book can be combined into nourishing, appetizing and satisfying meals.

SEASONAL MENUS FOR FAMILY MAIN MEALS
SPRING

Creamy Oatmeal and Dulse Soup (p. 30)

Sunflower and Almond Roast (p. 39)
Lightly steamed spring greens
Dill Pickle (p. 80)

Cream of Carrot Soup with Parsley Sprigs (p. 26)

Scalloped Potatoes (p. 42)
Coleslaw (p. 74)

SUMMER

Corn Chowder with watercress garnish
(p. 24)

Cauliflower Crusty (p. 41)
Boiled Brown Rice (p. 37)
Blanched baby carrots
Nori Condiment (p. 87)

Genmai Miso Soup with Lemon Wedges
(p. 23)

Oriental Succotash (p. 46)
Cooked millet (p. 37)
Blanched cauliflower in brown rice vinegar

AUTUMN

Rich Lentil Soup (p. 29)

Millet Soufflé (p. 55)
Oriental Arame and Cabbage (p. 44)
Radish Flowers in Umeboshi Vinegar (p. 81)

Pumpkin Purée Soup with Watercress
Garnish (p. 27)

Autumn Barley Stew (p. 48)
Toasted Flaked Almonds and lightly
steamed green beans
Crunchy Carrot and Beetroot Salad Garnish
(p. 75)

WINTER

Kombu and Ginger Broth (p. 22)

Stir-fry Vegetables and Brown Rice (p. 43)
Aduki Bean Sauce (p. 92)
Sauerkraut (p. 80)

Miso Broth with barley and vegetables and
spring onion garnish (p.23)

Buckwheat Savoury (p. 56)
Aduki Beans and Onion Sauce (p. 92)
Lightly steamed cauliflower
Dill Pickle (p. 80)

DINNER PARTY MENUS
SPRING

Clear Miso and Wakame Broth (p. 23)

Lentil Pâté (p. 32) served on rye toast triangles

Fruit and Vegetable Curry (p. 53)
Brown rice
Coleslaw with yogurt (p. 74)
Glazed Onions (p. 39)

Apple and Nut Crumble (p. 97)

SUMMER

Scandinavian Summer Soup (p. 23)

Celery, Wild Rice and Pecan Ring (p. 76)
Meatless Savoury Loaf (p. 63)
Dill Pickle (p. 80)

Brown Sugar Pavlova (p. 98)
Fresh Fruit Salad (p. 94)

AUTUMN

Mediterranean Fish Soup (p. 31)

Millet Croquettes (p. 70)
Boiled brown rice
Tremendously Tropical Sauce (p. 91)
Crunchy Carrot and Beetroot Salad (p. 75)
Broccoli and Walnuts (p. 40)

Buckwheat Crêpes (p. 108)
with Poached Autumn Fruits (p. 101)

WINTER

Cauliflower Purée Soup and Watercress
Garnish (p. 25)

Fresh River Trout and Almonds (p. 65)
Boiled potatoes
Lightly steamed broccoli

Thuri's Iceland Pie (p. 99)

CHRISTMAS MENUS

CHRISTMAS LUNCH

Mushroom Consommé (p. 25)

Roast turkey with Kinloch Haggis (p. 86) and Chestnut Stuffing (p. 86)
Chestnut Rice (p. 52)
Baked jacket potatoes
Lightly steamed Brussels sprouts and green peas
Chestnut sauce and cranberry sauce

Peaches in brandy or Fresh Fruit Salad (p. 94)

Coffee or grain coffee and Dreamy Truffles (p. 119)

CHRISTMAS TEA

Sautéed mushrooms in lemon juice and cream sauce

Baked Stuffed Marrow (p. 45) or boiled ham
Coleslaw (p. 74)
Carrot and Beetroot Salad (p. 75)
Plain boiled rice

Christmas Pudding (p. 98) with Brandy Sauce (p. 102)

Mince pies (p. 108) and Christmas Cake (p. 116)

FESTIVE SEASON DINNER PARTY MENUS

DINNER MENU 1

Mushroom Consommé (p. 25)

Roast capon with Apricot and Almond Stuffing (p. 86)
Chestnut Rice (p. 52)
Baked jacket potatoes
Lightly steamed Brussels sprouts

Mincemeat Tart (p. 108) with cream (optional)

Grain coffee and Dreamy Truffles (p. 119)

DINNER MENU 2

Cauliflower Soup (p. 25)

Baked Salmon on a Bed of Rice (p. 66)
Boiled potatoes
Lightly steamed broccoli
Cucumber Pickle (adapt p. 80)

Cheesecake (p. 100)

Coffee with Mince Pies (p. 108) and Dreamy Truffles (p. 119)

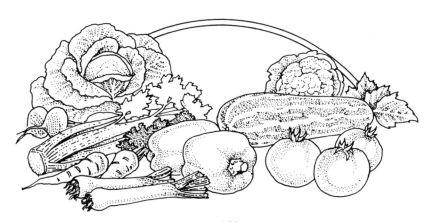

APPENDIX 1

WHEAT-FREE DIET

Many packeted and tinned foods contain *wheat*. Therefore read *all* food labels and check the ingredients listed.

Avoid:

All breads, buns, cookies, scones, pancakes, biscuits, cakes, pastries, certain oatcakes, non-rye crispbreads and rusks etc., made with, or including, wheat – refined or wholewheat – wheatgerm, bran, etc.

All breakfast cereals containing wheat, wheatgerm or bran. This includes some muesli cereals, all wheat cereals and bran cereals.

All thickeners in soups, stews, gravies, also many gravy flavourers, as a number of these are based on wheat.

All processed and tinned meats such as corned beef, sausages, beefburgers and hamburgers, black pudding, etc. which may contain cereal and/or MSG.

All foods containing monosodium glutamate (MSG).

All battered and breaded foods, e.g. fish fingers, and flour-based sauces such as cauliflower cheese, white fish in parsley sauce, chicken supreme, etc.

All products containing 'food starch' or 'wheat starch' such as some salad creams, stock cubes, ice cream, etc.

Milk puddings containing refined flour or semolina.

Spaghetti, macaroni and other pastas.

Bulghur (cracked wheat), cous-cous, spelt (ancient wheat).

Some ready-made mustards. Wholegrain mustards do not usually contain flour.

Some chocolates and other sweets.

Some instant coffees and malted milks.

Some alcoholic beverages, such as beer, whisky, gin and vodka.

(Wine, brandy and malt whisky do not contain wheat.)

The following are recommended alternatives to the foods which should be avoided on a 'wheat-free' diet.

Wholegrain cereal foods:

Home-made and bought breads, cakes and biscuits made from barley, rye, oats, brown rice and organically-grown wholewheat.

Rice bran, soya bran, oat bran and oatgerm. Puffed rice cakes (salted or unsalted) and rice crackers (check for MSG). Made from whole brown rice, these biscuits are both wheat-free and gluten-free.

Rye crispbreads (check ingredients).

Oatcakes (check ingredients).

Ask your local bakeries, supermarkets and health food shops to stock wheat-free products:

Porridges made from oatmeal, oat flakes and oat-based cereals.

Porridges made from barley kernels, brown rice and millet.

Puffed brown rice and puffed millet cereals, home-made pop-corn and wheat-free muesli. Use organically-grown grains whenever possible.

Thickeners:

When making gravies and sauces, try the wholegrain flours mentioned above, also potato flour, soya flour, arrowroot, kuzu and agar-agar. Try gravy unthickened.

Seasonings:

Sea salt, sesame salt (gomasio), tamari (wheat-free), and shoyu soya sauces, barley miso, various brands of yeast extract, mustard seed, fresh and dried herbs and pepper.

Animal produce:

Fresh lean meats, poultry, fish and shell-fish, eggs, milks and cheeses.

Pulse products:

Pulses, for example, split and whole peas, aduki beans, mung beans (for sprouting also), chick peas, brown, green and split lentils, black-eyed beans, soya milk, soya bean spreads, miso, tamari/shoyu soya sauce, tofu (soya bean curd).

Nuts and seeds:

Almonds, hazelnuts, walnuts, pecans.

Sunflower, sesame and pumpkin seeds, and seed spreads.

Sweets:

Check health food shops and super-markets for oat bars, carob, dried fruit snacks, sesame snaps. These are not recommended for daily use.

Pastas:

100% soba buckwheat noodles, potato noodles and some brown rice noodles.

Hot and cold beverages:

Roasted grain 'coffees', mild low-tannin teas and herbal tisanes such as weak infusions of elder flower, lime blossom and lemon balm.

Still and sparkling bottled waters.

Baking aids:

Cream of tartar, bicarbonate of soda, baker's yeast.

APPENDIX 2

MACROBIOTIC EATING GUIDE

1) Take at least 50 per cent by volume cooked of every meal as whole cereal grains, prepared by a variety of cooking methods. Whole cereal grains include brown rice, whole rye, barley, millet, oats, buckwheat etc. N.B., we are avoiding wheat, unless it has been organically-grown.

2) Have one or two small bowls of soup each day, lightly seasoned with miso (fer-mented soya bean paste), shoyu or tamari (traditional additive-free soya sauces). Both miso and soya sauce are rich in minerals, trace elements, vitamins and enzymes which aid digestion. Vary the soup recipes and include a selection of seasonal vegetables and seaweeds plus or minus pulses and grains.

3) Make vegetables about 20 to 30 per cent (2 to 3 tablespoons) of each main meal,

serving two-thirds of them cooked in various ways, such as sautéing, steaming, boiling and baking, and up to one-third as raw salad. Mayonnaise and commercial dressings should be avoided. Potatoes, including sweet potatoes and yams, tomatoes, aubergines, asparagus, spinach, beets, avocados and other tropical vegetables should be avoided or eaten only occasionally, unless you live in a tropical region.

4) From 10 to 15 per cent (1 to 1½ tablespoons with each main meal) of daily food intake should be provided by cooked pulses and seaweed. Suggested pulses for daily use are aduki beans, chick peas, brown or green lentils and black beans, with other varieties for occasional use. Seaweeds such as dulse (sloke or laver), carragheen (Irish or sea moss), nori (greenlaver or sea lettuce), kombu (kelp), wakame, arame and agar-agar can be prepared in a variety of ways. Pulse and seaweed dishes are best flavoured with a moderate amount of sea salt or tamari/shoyu soya sauce.

5) If wished, a small amount (3 oz/85g) of white fish (e.g. haddock, sole, whiting) may be eaten once or twice a week, varying the method of cooking. While meat, poultry, eggs and dairy products are not entirely excluded, they are not recommended for general use.

6) Include a seasonal fruit dessert two to three times a week as liked. For general use, choose fruits grown in the local climatic zone. Thus if you live in a temperate zone (a four-season climate), avoid, or eat only occasionally, tropical and semi-tropical fruits such as oranges, grapefruit, pineapple, coconut, mango, papaya, banana and avocado. This advice makes particular sense when one considers that the tropical and semi-tropical fruits available in the UK are intensively farmed, sprayed with insecticides, fumigants and fungicides and are generally picked unripe and then ripened artificially prior to sale. There are many instances of

people who are unable to eat imported fruits without suffering from digestive disorders (flatulence, diarrhoea, etc.) but have no such symptoms when eating the same fruit, sun-ripened, in its country of origin.

Fruit juice is not advised except for occasional consumption in very hot weather. Thirst is often best satisfied by sipping a hot, unsweetened drink (see page 122).

7) Between-meal eating and snacking is not advised but roasted seeds and nuts, dried fruits and roasted cooked pulses make enjoyable supplementary foods.

8) Recommended beverages include non-stimulant 'teas' and 'coffees' low in or free of tannin and caffeine, such as bancha twig tea, Luaka tea, dandelion root coffee (not the instant variety), cereal grain coffees made from barley and/or rye with or without chicory, as well as any mild herbal teas such as linden or lime flower.

FOODS BEST AVOIDED FOR IMPROVED HEALTH

These include:

Fruit juices, soda, artificial drinks and beverages;

White sugar, syrup, saccharine and other artificial sweeteners;

All chemicalized food such as coloured, preserved, sprayed and chemically treated foods, all refined, polished grains and their derivatives, and mass-produced, industrialized food, including all canned foods and commercially frozen foods.

Food accessories, e.g. bottled and packet sauces and vinegar.

FOODS BEST REDUCED CONSIDERABLY FOR IMPROVED HEALTH

These include:

Meat, animal fat, eggs, poultry, dairy foods including butter, milk, cream, commercial, flavoured yogurt, cheeses and margarines;

Tropical and semi-tropical fruits;

Coffee, tea and aromatic, stimulant teas such as mint, spice and fruit teas and alcoholic beverages;

Muscovado sugar, honey, molasses, rice honey and barley malt;

Hot spices, aromatic and stimulant food, such as curries and chillies.

ADDITIONAL SUGGESTIONS

1. Cooking oil should be of vegetable origin and should always be cold-pressed. Use good quality sesame, sunflower, safflower and corn oils in moderate volume.
2. Salt should be unrefined sea salt. All seasonings are best added during cooking and used sparingly.
3. Choose the best quality food available. The best organically/ biodynamically grown produce looks and tastes better than its alternatives as you will soon discover. You will be getting real value for your money.
4. Always remember to *chew your food well.*

Take time to eat and enjoy your meals. A small amount of well-prepared food is much more beneficial than a large quantity. Over-consumption of even recommended foods destroys the beneficial properties.

5. Dairy foods (although some are more balanced than others) are not recommended as anything other than 'pleasure foods' for occasional party use, as they are mucus-forming, particularly in a damp climate, and are poorly digested by many people who lack the required digestive enzymes beyond infancy.
6. As far as possible eat whole, unrefined, unadulterated (unsprayed, artificial additive-free) food.

You are advised to have a regular pattern of eating, e.g. two to three times per day, taking as much as you want, provided that the proportion is correct and chewing is thorough. Avoid eating for approximately three hours before sleeping. For advice on what and when to drink, see A Matter of Thirst on page 122.

APPENDIX 3

SOURCES OF NUTRIENTS

Protein:

From animal sources – meat, poultry, fish, seafood, eggs, milk, cheese, yogurt;

From vegetable sources – nuts, seeds, pulses (peas, beans, lentils, peanuts), grains.

To obtain the full benefit of vegetable proteins, combine ingredients as advised in the recipes and as follows:

1. Wholegrain cereals (such as brown rice, barley, oats, rye, organically-grown wheat, corn [maize] and millet) with peas, beans or lentils.
2. Wholegrain cereals with peanuts and milk or cheese.
3. Wholegrain cereals with sesame seeds

and soya beans, or soya milk.
4. Brown rice with sesame seeds.
5. Wholegrain cereals with brewer's yeast.
6. Pulses (peas, beans, lentils) with wholegrain cereals, nuts and seeds (especially sesame seeds).
7. Pulses with wholegrain cereals and milk or cheese.
8. Peanuts with sesame seeds and soya beans.
9. Peanuts and sunflower seeds.
10. Leafy green vegetables and mushrooms with wholegrain cereals and nuts or seeds.

Carbohydrates: Refined white sugar and white flour products are the commonly used sources of carbohydrate, which acts as an energy source in the diet. These products, however, are not recommended, as they lack the fibre and vitamin content of wholegrain cereals, pulses and fruits, which are more desirable sources of carbohydrate for energy needs and body maintenance.

Wholegrain cereals, breads and flour products, organically-grown whenever possible; brown rice, millet, barley, oats, rye, wheat, maize/corn, buckwheat (used as a grain, though classed as a seed);

Pulses – peas, beans and lentils;

Fresh and dried fruits, fruit juices and vegetables;

Maple syrup, brown rice syrup, barley malt and honey;

Unrefined sugars such as Barbados, Muscovado and molasses treacle;

Jams and jellies made with unrefined sugar or apple juice concentrate;

Sweets and chocolate.

N.B. All sugars, and sweetened foods and drinks, should be used sparingly, if used at all.

Fats: These are a concentrated source of energy and should be used sparingly, whether of animal or vegetable origin. Vegetable oils and fats are free from the cholesterol found in animal fats. Hard vegetable fats have no benefit over animal fats and, along with soft margarines, are highly processed products. Use butter and margarine sparingly, avoid deep-fried food, and when shallow-frying use cold-pressed oils. These contain vitamin E, a naturally-occurring antioxidant, which prevents rancidity.

Fats include: butter, margarine, cream, cheeses, fresh and dried milks, full fat yogurt, ice cream, oily fish (tuna, sardines, trout, herring, salmon), egg yolk (egg white is fat-free), fat on meat and in meat (in particular sausages, luncheon meats and hamburgers).

Always check margarine ingredients if following a dairy-free or milk-free diet; use only those brands which do *not* contain milk whey or milk solids. Low-fat milks, yogurts and cheese are available, which contain the same protein and calcium as the full-fat products. They can be useful in adult low-fat diets but should not be used for children under 5 years of age, in place of whole milk or infant formulas, as the low-fat products lack the fat-soluble vitamins, A and D, and have a more concentrated protein and calcium content.

SOURCES OF VITAMINS

Fat-soluble vitamins

Vitamin A: Liver, kidney, heart, butter, fortified margarine, egg yolk, oily fish and fish liver oils (cod, halibut), cheese, milk, parsley*, carrots, carrot tops, spinach, watercress, broccoli and other leafy greens, alfalfa sprouts, red peppers, swede, pumpkin, cantaloupe melon (orange flesh), apricots, peaches, nectarines, watermelon, mangoes.

Vitamin D: Direct sunlight on the skin stimulates the production of vitamin D by the body.
Liver, butter, fortified margarine, oily fish and fish liver oils, egg yolk, milk, cheeses, cream, cod roe, fortified soya milk. Traces have also been found in seaweeds.

Vitamin E: Vegetable, nut and seed oils (especially the 'cold-pressed' varieties). Wheatgerm, wholegrain cereals and flours, egg yolk, pulses, leafy green vegetables, nuts and seeds.

Vitamin K: Leafy green vegetables – kale, cabbage, spinach, watercress, etc., yellow vegetables and fruits, tubers (potatoes), seeds, tomatoes, egg yolk, soya bean oil and alfalfa.

Water-soluble vitamins

Vitamin B complex (B_1 thiamine; B_2 riboflavin; B_3 nicotinic acid; B_6 pyridoxine): Fish, liver, kidney, pork, poultry, wholegrains and wholegrain flour products, pulses, especially soya beans, peanuts, yeast and yeast extract seasonings, brewer's yeast, both powder and tablets, yogurt, milk, cheeses, seeds (sunflower, sesame, pumpkin), walnuts, chestnuts, leafy green vegetables.

Folic acid: Liver, kidney, leafy green vegetables, pulses, wholegrain cereals, cow's milk (but not goat's or sheep's milk), brewer's yeast, both powder and tablets.

Vitamin B_{12}: Cheese, milk, eggs, meat (particularly heart and liver), fish, poultry, some fortified soya products and fortified yeast extracts. Traces of B_{12} have been found in miso, tamari/shoyu soya sauce and seaweeds, but as this may not be sufficient for the body's needs, those avoiding *all* animal produce in their diets are advised to take a daily vitamin B_{12} supplement or supplemented food. The estimated daily requirement for a healthy adult is 0.3 micrograms.

Vitamin C: Leafy green vegetables, sprouted seeds (alfalfa, bean sprouts and grain sprouts), okra, citrus fruits (oranges, lemons, grapefruit, limes), papaya, mango, strawberries, blackcurrants, raspberries, cantaloupe melon, rosehips, sauerkraut (salt-pickled cabbage), sweet peppers, parsley and potatoes.

Note: Leafy green vegetables include: cress and watercress, lettuce, Chinese leaves, broccoli, cabbage, cauliflower and cauliflower greens, Brussels sprouts, spinach, kale, turnip tops and carrot tops.

*The vegetable and fruit sources contain carotene, the orange/red pigment which is converted to vitamin A by the body.

SOURCES OF MINERALS AND TRACE ELEMENTS

Calcium: Milk, cheese, yogurt, sardines, salmon (with bones as in the tinned product), leafy green vegetables, wholegrain cereals and flour products, eggs, brazil nuts, almonds, sesame seeds, sunflower seeds, pine kernels, seaweeds (kombu, etc.), dried fruits, Japanese twig tea.

Phosphorus: Fish, meat, molasses treacle,

eggs, leafy green vegetables, root vegetables (carrots, turnips), milk, cheese, nuts, dried apricots and prunes, pulses, wholegrain cereals.

Iron: Meats, especially red meats, liver, kidney, heart, egg yolk, pulses, wholegrain cereals and breads, dark green leafy vegetables (cabbage, spinach, broccoli, watercress), dried fruit (prunes, raisins, apricots), seaweeds such as dulse, kombu and kelp, sesame and pumpkin seeds, nuts, molasses treacle.
Note that iron absorption is enhanced by eating foods rich in vitamin C.

Magnesium: Brazil nuts, walnuts, almonds, wholegrain cereal and flour products, leafy green vegetables, dried fruit (figs, dates, apricots).

Manganese: Alfalfa, wholegrain cereals, pulses, leafy green vegetables, hazelnuts, chestnuts, almonds, avocado pears.

Sodium: Seasonings such as salt, miso, yeast extract, tamari/shoyu soya sauce, are all best used sparingly in cooking and not added at the table. Foods with added salt include cheeses, salted peanuts, cold meats, smoked foods, sodium additives in processed food (MSG), butter, potato crisps, bacon. Naturally occurring in many foods including cereals, eggs, celery, cucumber, green vegetables.

Potassium: Most foods, in particular, vegetables, seaweeds, bananas, apricots, brewer's yeast, both powder and tablets, tomatoes, fruit juices.

Iodine: Kelp and other seaweeds, leafy green vegetables grown in iodine-rich soils, peanuts, strawberries.

Zinc: Oysters, shrimps, dried peas, Cheddar cheese, beef, lamb, nuts, sardines, wholegrain cereals, beans, lentils, sunflower seeds.

MINERALS TO AVOID

A nutritious, high-fibre diet is the best

protection against environmental pollutants. Sea vegetables are specifically recommended as they contain substances which act as natural chelating agents for lead and other toxic metals, by gradually helping to remove these metals from the body.

Lead: Sources – lead piping, lead alloys used in soldering copper pipes (both affecting the water supply), car exhaust fumes, flaking lead paint, unlined seams of food cans.

Use a carbon water filter: the jug styles are economical and effective. But note that the filters must be changed as frequently as recommended by the manufacturers.

The effect of lead toxicity is more severe when the diet is deficient in essential nutrients.

If you live on a main road or in an industrial area, fine net curtains will catch some of the lead which enters through the windows.

Aluminium: Sources – aluminium or silver foil, aluminium cans or lined juice containers, kettles, pots and pans, teapots, pressure cookers, cake tins, roasting pans, baking trays and non-stick pans when the non-stick layer has been removed, tap-water containing aluminium flocculants. (See p. 137 for recommended cooking pots.)

Silico-aluminate is added to foods such as powdered non-dairy creamers, to stop them from caking.

Cadmium: Sources – industrial pollution, the burning of coal or oil, cigarette smoke, car exhaust fumes, food and water contamination (galvanized water pipes and black plastic pipes).

A diet rich in iron, zinc, vitamin C, fibre and milk proteins can help to decrease cadmium retention.

Fluorine/fluoride: No definite requirement for fluorine or fluoride has ever been established. It occurs naturally in tea, seafoods, in some vegetables (depending on the soil) and in some water sources. The average intake in this country from these sources exceeds the WHO recommended intake of 1 mg/day. There is therefore no need for the addition of artificial fluoride to public water supplies.

Copper: Sources – drinking water, particularly in areas where the water is 'soft' and acid, as in most parts of Scotland, copper pans, kettles, copper jewellery, henna dyes, swimming pool water treated with copper-containing algicides, certain water heaters, contraceptive pills, contraceptive copper coils and some multi-mineral pills.

N.B. Always use drinking water from a cold tap which has been allowed to run for 2-3 minutes.

Selenium: Sources – some shampoos, some photocopying machines.

Mercury: Sources – tinned tuna fish (has been linked with mercury 'scares' over the past few years), fish from rivers polluted with factory effluent (e.g. paper mills), some weed killers, dental amalgam used for fillings, grass seeds and other seeds treated with mercury powder.

APPENDIX 4

EQUIPPING THE KITCHEN

To the non-cook, or the new cook, the range of kitchen gadgetry seems endless. Each dish appears to require its own type of knife, grater or cooking pot to guarantee success. In reality, a set of well-chosen basic utensils, containers and cookware will be sufficient for most everyday needs.

Electrically-operated equipment is undoubtedly labour-saving and effective, but if you have reached a pitch of living where the microwave and the deep-freeze are your only means of survival, or where no meal is made without the use of some electrical device, then perhaps it is time to re-think that lifestyle.

It is possible to produce fast food from wholesome ingredients using the minimum of time, energy (your own and the planet's) and equipment.

COOKING POTS

The heavier the pot, enamelled or cast iron, the better the distribution of heat, the lower the cooking temperature required and the tastier the food. Weight, however, is a problem for many with painful hand joints and so a compromise must often be made. Choose stainless steel, glass or enamel-coated pots, and always check that lids fit well. Whenever possible, avoid aluminium, copper and non-stick varieties, especially in soft water areas.

A stainless steel *vegetable steamer* is a useful item. The adjustable type fits a variety of pot sizes.

A *frying pan* can be used for the dry-roasting of cereal grains, nuts and seeds, and is good for the occasional quick, low-fat method of cooking stir-fried vegetables, fish and rice. The oriental wok is designed specially for low-fat, instant meals.

A *pressure cooker* is not an essential but does shorten the cooking time of grains, pulses and vegetables. Be sure to buy a stainless steel version.

A selection of *ovenproof casseroles* with lids double as serving dishes.

A fine-gauge stainless steel *sieve* is useful for rinsing grains, seeds and pulses.

Wooden spoons, spatulas and *stirring sticks* (the Scottish *spurtle* or oriental *chopsticks*) are effective in use. Wooden implements are quieter to use than metal – a much appreciated consideration, not just a faddy idea.

Heatproof glass or *stainless steel mixing bowls* can double as storage dishes for leftovers or fresh food.

A small *plastic filter funnel* is useful for transferring liquids from larger containers into smaller bottles (buying soya sauce, apple juice, etc. in larger quantities tends to be more economical).

A *food processor, liquidizer, hand-operated food mill* or *suribachi/surikoji* (the Japanese equivalent of the *mortar and pestle* with a grooved interior) are effective in grinding roasted nuts and seeds, making purées or blending ingredients for sauces or salad dressings. Whichever type you use will depend on your ability to use it, and preference. If possible, choose the hand methods for economy and the best results.

BAKING

Loaf tins and a *baking sheet* are basics, with round cake tins for special use. Whether you intend to bake or not, a *wire cooling rack* and *wooden pot stand* are invaluable.

A *pastry brush* is the ideal way to apply a thin covering of oil to a pot base for shallow frying.

CUTTING AND CHOPPING

A well constructed *vegetable chopping knife* makes all the difference to the appearance and taste of your vegetable dishes. A blunt knife is frustrating to use and dangerous, so keep all knives well sharpened using an *oilstone* (the safest way to sharpen a knife). Other useful knives include one with a *serrated edge*, a *fruit knife* and a *bread knife*. A *vegetable brush* is an efficient way to clean vegetables without removing the peel.

A *free-standing grater* with a variety of surfaces and a *board* of durable hardwood are good investments and can be used for all chopping purposes. Most cooks acquire a variety of wooden boards in order to prevent the strong onion and garlic oils, which linger on a vegetable chopping board, from affecting the taste of breads or fruit.

A small hand-operated *grain mill* to

provide really fresh flavour from organically-grown wholegrains is worth considering if you intend to make your own bread. The difference in flavour has to be tasted to be believed.

CHOICE OF COOKER

For efficiency and satisfaction the solid fuel stoves, reminiscent of farmhouse kitchens, give the best results. Small woodburning stoves are becoming increasingly popular as they provide economical room heat whilst offering enough cooking space for one or two pots – ideal for winter stews and casseroles.

Most professional cooks prefer gas to electricity, and for controllable, gentle cooking, the gas flame certainly is the better choice. Microwave cooking is not recommended here.

FOOD STORAGE

Wholegrains and pulses keep almost indefinitely in cool, dry and pest-free containers. Once cracked or ground into flour, grains are best used immediately or within a short space of time, so buy flour and wholegrain flakes in small quantities from a shop that has a rapid turnover, to ensure freshness, especially in warm weather.

Nuts and seeds lose their flavour and turn rancid if kept too long. Store either in a cool, dark place with a well-fitting lid on the container or refrigerate, and do not grind or chop until ready to use.

It pays to buy good quality, fresh vegetables on a regular (daily) basis if at all possible. Bruised fruit is no saving. Aim for quality, not quantity.

Appendix 5

Cutting Styles for Vegetables and Special Preparations

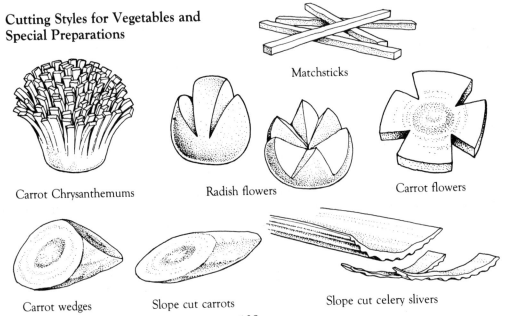

Matchsticks

Carrot Chrysanthemums

Radish flowers

Carrot flowers

Carrot wedges

Slope cut carrots

Slope cut celery slivers

CARROT FLOWERS

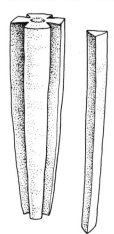

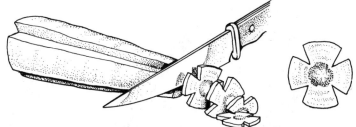

Top, tail and scrub carrots.

Remove a triangular wedge from four sides of the carrot then slice horizontally into ⅛″ to ¼″ 'flowers'.

Blanch 'flowers' in boiling water for 2-3 minutes then drain and cool and use to decorate Rice Balls, Pâté dishes, Grain & Bean loaves.

ONION CHRYSANTHEMUMS

Simmer to soften

petals open

push down with fingers to open out petals further.

BROWN RICE BALLS

Bowl of soft cooked rice

Form into rice ball by compressing in hands and rotating.

Wrap rice ball in nori

or

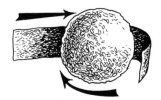

use strips of nori to wrap round centre of rice ball.

MAKING SUSHI

Press to make indentation and fill with pickles or raw vegetables.

Start to roll the Nori over the rice and use the sushi mat to firmly press the roll into a log shape. Dampen the top edge of Nori to seal the roll.

Use a sharp knife to slice the roll into rounds – wet the blade of the knife for an even cut.

Arrange the rounds on a serving plate.

FROM BEANBAG TO BEANSPROUTS

Beans or Grains

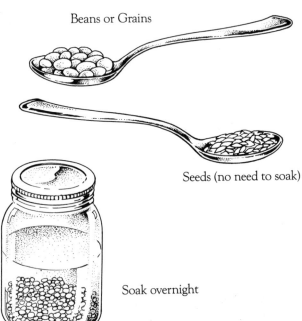

Seeds (no need to soak)

Soak overnight

Rubber band

Rinse and drain through muslin top. Place in a dark airy cupboard. Rinse and drain twice daily for 3-4 days.

On the last day of sprouting place jar in sunlight for extra vitamins. When ready to eat, cover and store in a cool place and use within 1-2 days.

An instant salad or nourishing snack will always be ready for use if you keep wholegrains, seeds and legumes (peas, beans and whole lentils) at different stages of sprouting.

Try Spicy Radish and Fenugreek, Refreshing Alfalfa, Crunchy Mungbeans and Sweet sprouted barley, rye or oats.

APPENDIX 6

FURTHER READING

Apart from the wheat-free aspect, the ideas expressed in this book are not new. For those of our readers who may wish to read more widely on the subject of diets and health, the following books are suggested as additional background material. This list is by no means exhaustive, but these books have been picked because a number of the ideas in them are similar to our own. The major point of difference lies in the fact that most of their authors have not appreciated the problems which we have encountered with commercially-grown wheat. Bearing this in mind, you may find in them some valuable additional information, ideas and explanations.

Food for Thought, Dr Saul Miller (Spectrum

Books, Prentice Hall Inc., New Jersey, 1979).

Nutrition and Health, Sir Robert McCarrison (McCarrison Press, 1982).

Problems with Meat, John A. Scharffenberg, MD (Woodbridge Press Publishing Company, California, 1979).

The Saccharine Disease, T. L. Cleave (John Wright and Sons Ltd., 1974).

Eating and Allergy, Robert Eagle (Thorsons, 1986).

Laurel's Kitchen, Laurel Robertson (Routledge and Kegan-Paul, 1979).

The Book of Wholemeals, A Colbin (Autumn Press, 1982).

Nature's Foods, Karen Betteridge and Peter Deadman (Unicorn Books, 1973).

The Book of Macrobiotics, Michio Kushi (Japan Publications Inc., 1977).

Soil and Civilization, Edward Hyams (John Murray, 1976).

Cooking with Care and Purpose, Rudolph Ballentine, MD (The Himalayan International Institute, Philadelphia, 1978).

Food and Drink in Britain, C. Anne Wilson (Penguin, 1984)

Various titles in the *Health Food Cooking Series* by Mala Young (David and Charles, 1981).

The Medicine Men, A Guide to Natural Medicines, John Lloyd Fraser (Thomas Methuen, 1981).

Green Pharmacy: A History of Herbal Medicine Barbara Griggs (Norman and Hobhouse, 1982).

Herbs and Spices, Jan Kybal (Hamlyn, 1980).

Raw Energy, Leslie and Susannah Kenton (Century, 1984).

The Right Food For Your Kids, Louise Templeton (Century 1984).

Food Combining For Health, Doris Grant (Thorsons, 1985).

Wheatless Cooking, Lynette Coffey (David and Charles, 1985).

Goodbye to Arthritis, Patricia Byrivers (Century, 1985).

The Food Scandal, Caroline Walker and Geoffrey Cannon (Century, 1984). London, 1985.

INDEX